LET'S GET TOGETHER

8 sessions on launching our small group

by Julie A. Gorman

VICTOR BOOKS®

A DIVISION OF SCRIPTURE PRESS PUBLICATIONS INC.
USA CANADA ENGLAND

Recommended Dewey Decimal Classification: 301.402
Suggested Subject Heading: SMALL GROUPS

Library of Congress Catalog Card Number: 91-65458
ISBN: 0-89693-299-0

1   2   3   4   5   6   7   8   9   10 Printing / Year   95   94   93   92   91

VICTOR BOOKS
A division of SP Publications, Inc.
          Wheaton, Illinois 60l87

LET'S GET TOGETHER

CONTENTS

PURPOSE: To experience a principle of small groups in each session.

INTRODUCTION

Let's Get Together is for people who want to know more about how small groups function. An in-depth Leader's Guide is included at the back of the book with suggested time guidelines to help you structure your emphases. Each of the 8 sessions contains the following elements:

❏ **GroupSpeak**—quotes from group members that capsulize what the session is about.

❏ **Getting Acquainted**—activities or selected readings to help you begin thinking and sharing from your life and experiences about the subject of the session. Use only those options that seem appropriate for your group.

❏ **Gaining Insight**—questions and in-depth Bible study help you gain principles from Scripture for life-related application.

❏ **Growing By Doing**—an opportunity to practice the Truth learned in the Gaining Insight section.

❏ **Going The Second Mile**—a personal enrichment section for you to do on your own.

❏ **Growing As A Leader**—an additional section in the Leader's Guide for the development and assessment of leadership skills.

❏ **Pocket Principles**—brief guidelines inserted in the Leader's Guide to help the Group Leader learn small group leadership skills as needed.

❏ **Session Objectives**—goals listed in the Leader's Guide that describe what should happen in the group by the end of the session.

IS THIS YOUR FIRST SMALL GROUP?

'smol grüp: A limited number of individuals assembled together having some unifying relationship.

Kris'chən
'smol grüp: 4–12 persons who meet together on a regular basis, over a determined period of time, for the shared purpose of pursuing biblical truth. They seek to mature in Christ and become equipped to serve as His ministers in the world.

Picture Your First Small Group.

List some words that describe what you want your small group to look like.

What Kind Of Small Group Do You Have?
People form all kinds of groups based on gender, age, marital status, and so forth. There are advantages and disadvantages to each. Here are just a few:

❑ **Same Age Groups** will probably share similar needs and interests.

❏ **Intergenerational Groups** bring together people with different perspectives and life experiences.

❏ **Men's or Women's Groups** usually allow greater freedom in sharing and deal with more focused topics.

❏ **Singles or Married Groups** determine their relationship emphases based on the needs of a particular marital status.

❏ **Mixed Gender Groups** (**singles and/or couples**) stimulate interaction and broaden viewpoints while reflecting varied lifestyles.

However, the most important area of "alikeness" to consider when forming a group is an **agreed-on purpose.** Differences in purpose will sabotage your group and keep its members from bonding. If, for example, Mark wants to pray but not play while Jan's goal is to learn through playing, then Mark and Jan's group will probably not go anywhere. People need different groups at different times in their lives. Some groups will focus on sharing and accountability, some on work projects or service, and others on worship. *Your small group must be made up of persons who have similar goals.*

How Big Should Your Small Group Be?
The **fewest** people to include would be **4.** Accountability will be high, but absenteeism may become a problem.

The **most** to include would be **12.** But you will need to subdivide regularly into groups of 3 or 4 if you want people to feel cared for and to have time for sharing.

How Long Should You Meet?
8 Weeks gives you a start toward becoming a close community, but doesn't overburden busy schedules. Count on needing three or four weeks to develop a significant trust level. The smaller the group, the more quickly trust develops.

Weekly Meetings will establish bonding at a good pace and allow for accountability. The least you can meet and still be an effective group is once a month. If you choose the latter, work at individual contact among group members between meetings.

You will need **75 minutes** to accomplish a quality meeting. The larger the size, the more time it takes to become a healthy group. Serving refreshments will add 20–30 minutes, and singing and/or prayer time, another 20–30 minutes. Your time duration may be determined by the time of day you meet and by the amount of energy members bring to the group. Better to start small and ask for more time when it is needed because of growth.

What Will Your Group Do?

To be effective, each small group meeting should include:

1. **Sharing**—You need to share who you are and what is happening in your life. This serves as a basis for relationship building and becomes a springboard for searching out scriptural truth.

2. **Scripture**—There must always be biblical input from the Lord to teach, rebuke, correct, and train in right living. Such material serves to move your group in the direction of maturity in Christ and protects from pooled ignorance and distorted introspection.

3. **Truth in practice**—It is vital to provide opportunities for *doing* the Word of God. Experiencing this within the group insures greater likelihood that insights gained will be utilized in everyday living.

Other elements your group may wish to add to these three are: a time of **worship, specific prayer** for group members, **shared projects,** a time to **socialize** and enjoy **refreshments,** and **recreation.**

ONE

Choices

GroupSpeak: *"Different people desire different things from a group. In a way, that was a shock to me because I knew what I wanted to get out of our group, and I assumed that everyone else wanted that, too. But that didn't turn out to be true. People choose to be in a group for different reasons."*

You Have A Choice!

Strawberry Creme?	Vanilla?	Cherry?
Chocolate Ripple?	Butter Brickle?	Peach?
Small?	Medium?	Large?
Ice Milk?	Yogurt?	Premium?

Our world knows the value of having a choice. Baskin Robbins created and built an empire on making available 31 flavors from which to choose. We choose the brand of coffee we drink and whether we want our cereal honey-sweetened, in circles, flakes, or nuggets. Most of us probably selected the car we drive on the basis of economy, color, model, accessories available, usefulness to your purposes.

Choices are a fun part of life. We enjoy the freedom of selection put under our control. Having a choice means we don't have to accept what we receive. It gives us a feeling of value

13

as well as a sense of responsibility. While we may "get what we ask for," we must also live with the choices we make.

Let's examine the choices involved in a small group as we meet together for the first time. We'll learn who we are in terms of our choices. We'll focus on what it means to be "chosen" and rejoice over God's choices. Finally, we'll look at what responsibilities go along with choices.

GETTING ACQUAINTED

Birds of a Feather

After your **Group Leader** designates three distinct areas of the room as **A, B,** and **C,** indicate your choice among the three options by moving to the appropriate area that represents your preference.

Do you prefer	A	B	C
a vacation at the	beach	mountains	desert/other

Where specifically do you like to go?

studying	Gospels	Epistles	Psalms

What's a favorite book/section?

living in the	city	suburbs	rural area

What do you like about your choice?

watching	comedy	drama	science fiction

Why did you make this choice?

eating food that is	salty	sweet	sour

And your favorite is?

14

| relaxing by | reading a book | exercising | taking a nap |

Why did you choose this?

| sitting in church | at the back | in the middle | at the front |

Why?

Did you notice some of the same people kept showing up in your group? Find someone who made some of the same selections as yourself and affirm him or her for making such wise choices!

GAINING INSIGHT

Understanding Choices
Life is filled with choices. List some choices you've made today.

Choices made this morning: Choices made this afternoon:
_____   _____
_____   _____
_____   _____
_____   _____
_____   _____

Turn to your neighbor and share at least five choices you've made today.

Choices are important for involvement in a small group. Our choices reveal who we are. Being in a small group community means we will be making choices based on our expectations and desires. We have chosen to be obedient to Jesus who has commanded us to relate to one another as His body, the church. He has called us to be the church, not just go to church. And becoming a part of a small group is one of the best ways to get involved in fulfilling that calling.

You have chosen to place yourself in a situation where it is highly probable that you will be called upon to grow and to join with others in putting the Word of God into practice.

Scripture Study
Let's examine what the Bible has to say about the formation of Jesus' small group—a group of 12 whose lives would be revolutionized by being together with Him as their leader. Read the following Scripture passage, noting those whom Jesus chose to become a part of His group.

[35]The next day John was there again with two of his disciples. [36]When he saw Jesus passing by, he said, "Look, the Lamb of God!"

[37]When the two disciples heard him say this, they followed Jesus. [38]Turning around, Jesus saw them following and asked, "What do you want?"

They said, "Rabbi," (which means Teacher), "where are You staying?"

[39]"Come," He replied, "and you will see."

So they went and saw where He was staying, and spent that day with Him. It was about the tenth hour.

[40]Andrew, Simon Peter's brother, was one of the two who heard what John had said and who had followed Jesus. [41]The first thing Andrew did was to find his brother Simon and tell him, "We have found the Messiah" (that is, the Christ). [42]And he brought him to Jesus.

Jesus looked at him and said, "You are Simon son of John. You will be called Cephas" (which, when translated, is Peter).

[43]The next day Jesus decided to leave for Galilee. Finding Philip, He said to him, "Follow me."

[44]Philip, like Andrew and Peter, was from the town of Bethsaida. [45]Philip found Nathanael and told him, "We have found the one Moses wrote about in the Law, and about

16

whom the prophets also wrote—Jesus of Nazareth, the son of Joseph."

⁴⁶"Nazareth! Can anything good come from there?" Nathanael asked.

"Come and see," said Philip.

⁴⁷When Jesus saw Nathanael approaching, He said to him, "Here is a true Israelite, in whom there is nothing false."

⁴⁸"How do You know me?" Nathanael asked.

Jesus answered, "I saw you while you were still under the fig tree before Philip called you."

⁴⁹Then Nathanael declared, "Rabbi, You are the Son of God; You are the King of Israel."

⁵⁰Jesus said, "You believe because I told you I saw you under the fig tree. You shall see greater things than that." ⁵¹He then added, "I tell you the truth, you shall see heaven open, and the angels of God ascending and descending on the Son of Man."

John 1:35-51

What choices did Jesus' followers make in this passage?

In what ways could the disciples' choices affect the rest of their lives?

It's energizing to be a chooser—to realize that the choices you make to pursue a relationship can impact the rest of your life. There is power in choosing—there is also responsibility.

17

In Jesus' day it was common for followers to choose their rabbi—a great teacher from whom they could learn the Law and after whom they could pattern their lives. Jesus, however, reversed the pattern. Even though Jesus' group members made choices, He was the ultimate Chooser and they the chosen ones. Let's read the following passages to see how Jesus was the ultimate Chooser.

¹³Jesus went up on a mountainside and called to Him those He wanted, and they came to Him. ¹⁴He appointed twelve—designating them apostles—that they might be with Him and that He might send them out to preach, ¹⁵and to have authority to drive out demons.

Mark 3:13-15

⁷⁰Then Jesus replied, "Have I not chosen you, the Twelve?"

John 6:70a

¹⁶"You did not choose Me, but I chose you and appointed you to go and bear fruit—fruit that will last. Then the Father will give you whatever you ask in My name."

¹⁹"If you belonged to the world, it would love you as its own. As it is, you do not belong to the world, but I have chosen you out of the world. That is why the world hates you."

John 15:16, 19

Think of a time when *you* were a chooser. How do you feel when you are the *chooser* in a situation?

How do you feel when you are the *one chosen?*

In what way are you (and the rest of the people in your small group) chosen?

On an all-star team, each member (even though he or she may come from differing backgrounds) looks at the teammates as valuable because they have been chosen. Each team member is there to represent a cause that unites them all. How many things do you share in common with others in this group?

GROWING BY DOING

Thanking The Chooser
Let's take a few minutes to pray and thank Jesus for choosing each member of our small group. He has placed us together, not by accident, but by design, so together we can build a relationship with Him and carry out His work in the world supporting each other. What are some things you appreciate about each person in the group?

Now let's talk about our choices. Let's share why we chose to belong to this group. What does this small group community need to become for it to be a satisfying group for you? What motivated you to want to be a part of this group?

GOING THE SECOND MILE

Group Checkup
Spend some time during the next few days thinking about your group. Complete the following statements that describe how you feel right now about why God chose for you to be a part of this group.

❑ Looks like these people will help me grow in_____ .
❑ I can find a sense of belonging here, especially with
_____ .
❑ I can have a ministry in this group by _____ .
❑ I'd like to get to know_____ .
❑ A person I can learn from is _____ .
❑ I felt supported by_____ .
❑ A member I identified with is_____ .
❑ Something I want to check up on next time is _____ .
❑ Someone I can encourage by contacting him or her before our next meeting is _____ .
❑ Parts of the group time I especially liked were_____ .

TWO

Commitments

GroupSpeak: *"Bible study? I thought this was going to be a sharing group. . . . I can only make it every other week — so don't look for me next week. . . . When he says sharing, he doesn't mean what I mean when I say sharing. . . . I didn't know we were supposed to read the chapter before coming. . . . How much longer do you think this group will continue to meet? . . . I wasn't aware we would have to take turns leading the prayer time."*

You Gotta' Wanna'

"I, John, take you, Mary. . . ."

"By signing this contract you choose to buy the motor vehicle on credit and agree to pay the total sale price in the amounts under the terms. . . ."

"In return for your services, the company agrees to supply you with the following benefits. . . ."

Commitments are a part of life. Relationships require commitment. Sometimes they are written, sometimes they are verbal, and sometimes they remain as unspoken expectations and desires. The latter may bring surprise and hurt to a

21

relationship because one person didn't know what the other person was thinking. Verbalizing commitments which express the disciplines or investments one is willing to make in a relationship increases the chances of the relationship surviving and growing. Think about the commitments you have in your life.

GETTING ACQUAINTED

Levels Of Importance

On each of the following continuums, place a **C** to identify the importance of commitment you had to that particular relationship or specific value when you were a child. Place a **Y** to identify where you placed the importance as a youth, and an **A** to show how you feel about committing to that person or value as an adult.

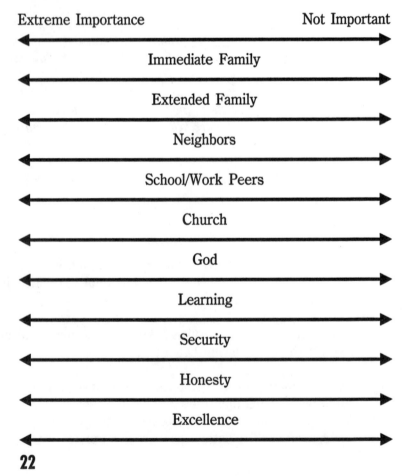

Extreme Importance   Not Important

⟵————————————————⟶
Immediate Family

⟵————————————————⟶
Extended Family

⟵————————————————⟶
Neighbors

⟵————————————————⟶
School/Work Peers

⟵————————————————⟶
Church

⟵————————————————⟶
God

⟵————————————————⟶
Learning

⟵————————————————⟶
Security

⟵————————————————⟶
Honesty

⟵————————————————⟶
Excellence

⟵————————————————⟶

What do you conclude about your commitments as you look over the continuums?

Shared Commitment

Read aloud **GroupSpeak.** Notice what these statements reveal about the importance of sharing commitments within a group right at the very start.

Each of the statements expresses confusion, disillusionment, or frustration growing out of unmet and unexpressed expectations which require accepting or declining responsibility. One statement expresses disappointment in the direction the group is going; its purpose wasn't clear.

Another statement points out that words do not mean the same thing to everyone. Not only do they have different explanations, but different intensities. A mother and child have totally different pictures in mind when the words, "clean your room" are uttered.

Leadership and responsibility need to be discussed before committing to a group. Requirements and responsibilities must be spelled out, including expectations in attending, in involvement, in the amount of time given, and in amount of effort to be exerted. Such things as beginning and ending the time of group meetings, regular attendance, expected contact with members between meetings, adopting a group project, providing refreshments—all need to be discussed so each of us can make a commitment or negotiate. This is called *covenanting* and requires at least two parties accepting agreed-upon terms.

Can you think of any times when you felt confused or uncomfortable in a group because you didn't know or hadn't agreed to the requirements of the group?

GAINING INSIGHT

Scripture Study

History is full of incidents where people wanted something so much, they were willing to pay a huge price to achieve it. Olympic years provide us with numerous examples. The national news picked up the story of Mark Wellman, a young man who lost the use of his legs in a climbing accident. Though a paraplegic, Mark wanted to climb El Capitan in Yosemite National Park. The world watched as this young man and his companion scaled 3,569 vertical feet up the face of this impressive granite fortress. Mark calculated that he used his arms to hoist himself the equivalent of 7,000 push-ups. He and his companion faced temperatures of 105 degrees and wind gusts that blew them 10 feet out from the rock. But they were committed! In the summer of 1989 they stood atop the massive challenge of El Capitan, their goal achieved.

In Scripture, the desire to please God was often accompanied by great personal costs. What characters in Scripture can you recall who paid a price to please God because of their commitment to Him?

Wanting to follow God's commands and to grow always involves disciplines or risks—often expressed in the price of obedience. Voluntary commitment that involves self-sacrifice is not necessarily popular today. It goes against the grain of personal fulfillment. Commitment means ultimate allegiance to another or to a cause that is greater than immediate personal gratification. Yet we are drawn to those who seem to have a purpose greater than themselves.

Chariots of Fire aroused an admiration within us as we saw Eric Liddel's commitment to a standard that was higher than his own self-fulfillment. Who can forget the Prince of Wales' shocking decision to "give up the throne for the woman I love" as he lived out his commitment to Wallis Simpson. What persons in history come to mind when you think of examples of commitment?

24

In today's climate of ease and self-gratification we find many don't have what it takes to work at a lasting alliance, to hang in with a difficult relationship, to stay with a group going through stretching times. There's always another group, another person, another cause where the problems won't be so draining and the cost not so high.

It was costly to commit to Jesus and to being in His small group. We hear His call to "follow Me," and our hearts beat with the excitement Peter and John must have experienced as they launched out on new adventures with this up-and-coming Rabbi.

But such commitment cost. Being committed to Jesus meant they were part of a group with people who were different from them. Jesus extended His invitation to a disdained publican who probably collected taxes for the coffers of Rome. To many, Matthew must have seemed an opportunist, out to make a buck at his own people's expense. And Matthew must have wondered why Jesus asked Simon — the passionate Zionist nationalist — to be a part of His group. A Zionist would be zealous to overthrow Roman rule in any way possible. Peter with his brashness must have been a memorable group member. What bound them together was their commitment to Jesus.

That commitment had its price tag. When the rich young ruler turned his back on following Jesus because the cost was too high, Peter reflected aloud on the price tag he and the other disciples had paid. Let's look at Mark 10:28-30.

²⁸Peter said to Him, "We have left everything to follow You!"

²⁹"I tell you the truth," Jesus replied, "no one who has left home or brothers or sisters or mother or father or children or fields for Me and the Gospel ³⁰will fail to receive a hundred times as much in this present age (homes, brothers, sisters, mothers, children, and fields — and with them, persecutions) and in the age to come, eternal life."

Mark 10:28-30

What do you think *everything* in verse 28 included?

What do you think commitment cost those who agreed to a discipling relationship with Jesus?

Note that the disciples could have stayed home and clung to what they had. But there is a cost in non-commitment also. It is costly to cling to the comfortable and safe. It is costly to refuse to obey. It is costly to choose to turn away. An old saying reminds us: "The saddest word from tongue or pen is simply this: it might have been." What "might have been" had Adam not chosen to disobey? What "might have been" had the rich young ruler followed through on Jesus' suggestion?

Peter again was confronted with the price of commitment in John 6. In this passage, Jesus declares to the crowd His divine nature and the absolute necessity of accepting Him for eternal life. Read the following Scripture passage.

57"Just as the living Father sent Me and I live because of the Father, so the one who feeds on Me will live because of Me."

60On hearing it, many of His disciples said, "This is a hard teaching. Who can accept it?"

61Aware that His disciples were grumbling about this, Jesus said to them, "Does this offend you? 62What if you see the Son of Man ascend to where He was before!"

66From this time many of His disciples turned back and no longer followed Him.

67"You do not want to leave too, do you?" Jesus asked the Twelve.

68Simon Peter answered Him, "Lord, to whom shall we go?

26

You have the words of eternal life. ⁶⁹We believe and know that you are the Holy One of God."

⁷⁰Then Jesus replied, "Have I not chosen you, the Twelve?"
John 6:57, 60-62, 66-70

What do these verses suggest about the price tag for commitment?

What hard teaching did Jesus give His followers in verse 62?

Why is it hard even for people today to hear and accept these words?

What do you think made the difference between those who left and those who stayed in verse 66?

Why do you think having to change affects commitment?

Why do you think Jesus asked the question in verse 67?

Study verses 68-69 and then, in your own words, tell the person beside you what Peter is saying.

Jesus' response in verse 70 is interesting because it reveals His commitment to the disciples. He chose them as His

Twelve, knowing all about them. He was committed to them as His own. His commitment to them and to His Father would cost Him His life.

Reaffirm Your Commitment
Knowing that Someone knows all about us and is committed to us brings feelings of security and value. Before we talk about our commitments to one another, let's reaffirm our commitment to Jesus and thank Him for His commitment to us.

 GROWING BY DOING

Writing Your Commitment
When commitments are made, words may be expressed. But commitment is primarily lived out in responsibilities we accept and carry out. When you take out a loan to buy a car, you agree to certain responsibilities—paying the amount agreed upon by a certain date, getting insurance, etc.

Likewise, in a small group it is helpful to talk over things we will expect of one another and responsibilities we will agree to. Since this is everyone's group we all need to share what we can or cannot be committed to.

What expectations do you have? If you were to write out your commitment to this small group, what things would you include?

Put a star beside the three items which you feel are of greatest importance in the realm of making commitments to one another within a small group community.

Let's go around the group with each person sharing one thing desired and what it is likely to cost.

Our Small Group Covenant
Use this space to summarize and record our agreed-upon covenant.

GOING THE SECOND MILE

Group Checkup
How do you feel about the covenant our small group designed?

❑ More than I expected
❑ Just right
❑ I can live with it
❑ I feel uncomfortable
❑ Excited

What is something you learned about the members of our group?

Did you learn something about yourself as you went through the process of designing a covenant? What was it?

What's one insight or promise from God that still keeps coming to mind from our study together?

What difference will that insight make in your response to the people in our group or your outlook on your week?

29

THREE

Relationships

GroupSpeak: *"My small group gave me the opportunity to share the way I was feeling about a situation in my life, something I probably wouldn't have shared with just anyone. It was a unique experience. I felt I could tell them how I really felt and they were so supportive."*

To Know Me Is To Love Me

Being the "real thing" is often promoted as desirable today. No phony facades can substitute for reality. But reality can be a scary thing.

What is real? On the surface, many of us appear to have our "act together." However, it is difficult to maintain that stance as we get close to people and they see us as we really are.

A bumper sticker proudly declares, "To know me is to love me," and something within us says, *Yes . . . if people understood me, they would find me lovable.* But then a voice whispers, *If people knew the real you, would they be surprised and shocked?* Most of us can identify with John Powell's best-seller, *Why I Am Afraid To Tell You Who I Am.* We want others to know us, but even more than that, we want others to know us and to accept us for who we are.

Being in a small group is a big step in the direction of being known and accepted. A small group is a climate for caring and for learning how to share with others. And the more we share and care for one another the more we become one.

Jesus had in mind that His followers would come to know each other as real persons and thus come to care for one another in a way that would cause the world to take notice. Real caring cannot begin until the real person is known.

GETTING ACQUAINTED

Trading Information

Divide into groups of four or six. Using the suggestions below, ask another group member to trade information with you. Make sure you trade within the same Level. Not all items need to be shared. This will enable us to learn more about others in our group at a level we choose to share.

Level 1
- ❑ Something I like about my family
- ❑ Something I detest
- ❑ A conviction of mine
- ❑ A pet peeve of mine
- ❑ A habit of mine
- ❑ How I felt about myself as a youth

Level 2
- ❑ Something I'm proud of
- ❑ Something I disliked about my family of origin
- ❑ A victory I've had
- ❑ What I like about me
- ❑ Where I see change in me
- ❑ How I feel about my role in my family

Level 3
- ❑ Something I fear
- ❑ A weakness of mine
- ❑ Something I struggle with
- ❑ Something I'd like to change about me
- ❑ Something that's hard for me to share
- ❑ How I feel about myself as a Christian

GAINING INSIGHT

Scripture Study

It was no accident that Jesus usually called His small group "the Twelve." He saw how the disciples complimented one another's strengths and weaknesses, and He sought to build them into a caring unit who knew each other well—faults and all. His desire was that the Twelve would be bonded not only to Him, but also to each other. Think about Jesus' time with the Twelve as you read the following passages.

³³**But when Jesus turned and looked at His disciples, He rebuked Peter. "Get behind Me, Satan!" He said. "You do not have in mind the things of God, but the things of men."** ³⁴**Then He called the crowd to Him along with His disciples and said: "If anyone would come after Me, he must deny himself and take up his cross and follow Me.** ³⁵**For whoever wants to save his life will lose it, but whoever loses his life for Me and for the Gospel will save it.** ³⁶**What good is it for a man to gain the whole world, yet forfeit his soul?** ³⁷**Or what can a man give in exchange for his soul?"**

Mark 8:33-37

⁴⁶**An argument started among the disciples as to which of them would be the greatest.** ⁴⁷**Jesus, knowing their thoughts, took a little child and had him stand beside Him.** ⁴⁸**Then He said to them, "Whoever welcomes this little child in My name welcomes Me; and whoever welcomes Me welcomes the one who sent Me. For he who is least among you all—he is the greatest."**

Luke 9:46-48

¹²**When He had finished washing their feet, He put on His clothes and returned to His place.** ¹³**"You call me 'Teacher' and 'Lord,' and rightly so, for that is what I am.** ¹⁴**Now that I, your Lord and Teacher, have washed your feet, you also should wash one another's feet."**

John 13:12-14

⁹**Jesus answered: "Don't you know Me, Philip, even after I have been among you such a long time? Anyone who has seen Me has seen the Father. How can you say, 'Show us the Father'?"**

33

¹⁰"Don't you believe that I am in the Father, and that the Father is in Me? The words I say to you are not just My own."

John 14:9-10

What did the Twelve do when they met together?

How did Jesus deal with conflicts in His small group?

What do you see Jesus doing to build trust and concern in the Twelve for each other?

The Book of Acts gives us a picture of the Twelve after Jesus returned to heaven. When the Holy Spirit came, He produced a church that was known for its care and togetherness. At a time when the church was recognized for its effectiveness and power, it was also marked by intense loving relationships where believers cared for and opened themselves up to one another. There was no place for isolated competitiveness. All shared in what God was doing and there was a mutuality of care and ministry.

Acts 2:42-47 is a newsreel of the life of first century believers. Let's read it together looking for evidences of trust and togetherness.

⁴²They devoted themselves to the apostles' teaching and to the fellowship, to the breaking of bread and to prayer. ⁴³Everyone was filled with awe, and many wonders and miraculous signs were done by the apostles. ⁴⁴All the believers were together and had everything in common. ⁴⁵Selling their possessions and goods, they gave to anyone as he had need. ⁴⁶Every day they continued to meet together in the temple courts. They broke bread in their homes and ate together with glad and sincere hearts, ⁴⁷praising God and enjoying the favor of all the people.

34

And the Lord added to their number daily those who were being saved.

Acts 2:42-47

How does this band of believers reflect togetherness and trust of one another?

What is appealing about this group of people?

Of course not everybody responded positively to the events described in this passage. Two of the apostles, Peter and John, became a target for the jealous Jews. After healing an outcast of society who begged for funds at the entrance to the temple, Peter and John were jailed overnight and warned "not to speak or teach at all in the name of Jesus" (Acts 4:18). They were both threatened if they persisted in their ministry. Facing this dilemma of threats versus carrying out their convictions, they returned to the group who had been "family" to them.

Let's read what took place in Acts 4:23-35.

²³On their release, Peter and John went back to their own people and reported all that the chief priests and elders had said to them. ²⁴When they heard this, they raised their voices together in prayer to God. "Sovereign Lord," they said, "You made the heaven and the earth and the sea, and everything in them. ²⁵You spoke by the Holy Spirit through the mouth of Your servant, our father David:

'Why do the nations rage and the peoples plot in vain?

²⁶The kings of the earth take their stand and the rulers gather together against the Lord and against His Anointed One.'

²⁷Indeed Herod and Pontius Pilate met together with the Gentiles and the people of Israel in this city to conspire

against Your holy servant Jesus, whom You anointed. [28]They did what Your power and will had decided beforehand should happen. [29]Now, Lord, consider their threats and enable Your servants to speak Your word with great boldness. [30]Stretch out Your hand to heal and perform miraculous signs and wonders through the name of Your holy servant Jesus."

[31]After they prayed, the place where they were meeting was shaken. And they were all filled with the Holy Spirit and spoke the word of God boldly.

[32]All the believers were one in heart and mind. No one claimed that any of his possessions was his own, but they shared everything they had. [33]With great power the apostles continued to testify to the resurrection of the Lord Jesus, and much grace was upon them all. [34]There were no needy persons among them. For from time to time those who owned lands or houses sold them, brought the money from the sales and put it at the apostles' feet, and it was distributed to anyone as he had need.

Acts 4:23-35

What qualities were present in this group ministry? What good principles did they exhibit?

Note that nobody made any laws concerning togetherness and sharing. These people did all this because they wanted to do it. Nowhere does the Scripture suggest that we all need to be exactly like this group in the things we share. This was their way of expressing their commitment to God and their love for one another.

Care Is A Personal Thing

Each of us has his or her own idea of what caring is. The more time we spend together with each other, the more likely we are to want to care for each other. It's important that we know what says "caring" to you. If we are to become

36

a caring group, what are some things that should be included from your viewpoint?

Take a look at the following suggested ways of caring. Which ones could we agree on for this group?

❑ Openly talk about reaching out to others
❑ Share honestly and freely
❑ Listen to others as they share
❑ Get together between group times
❑ Look for each other at church gatherings
❑ Write down concerns expressed by persons in the group and then follow up with a phone call
❑ Express appreciation for what persons do that encourage or help you
❑ Affirm positive traits or growth in each other
❑ Pray for each other

GROWING BY DOING

Caring For Us
What is an area of concern in your life right now? How could your group be supportive? What is something you have to offer to your group? Can you see a way in which what you have to offer could be helpful to another in the group or to the group as a whole? What could you invest in your group?

GOING THE SECOND MILE

Group Checkup
❑ What is one idea, person, or action that encouraged or supported you in your group time?
❑ What is something you invested in the group this time which you hadn't given before?
❑ What did you reveal about yourself so the group could know you?
❑ What did you pick up on that someone else was revealing?
❑ How do you plan to follow through on caring for the Body of Christ? Whom will you care for?

FOUR

Truth

GroupSpeak: *"It was in a small group that I first got excited about what's in the Bible. I saw people wrestling with issues in their lives and finding guidelines for how to resolve those issues as they studied Scripture. I'd always thought of Bible study as rather dry and extraneous to my life. But with everybody participating and sharing how Scripture related to their lives, I couldn't help but get enthused about learning biblical principles and study skills."*

What You Don't Know Can Hurt You

"So, what do you know?" is a common greeting in some parts of the country. Someone has said that a major goal of education is to know what you know and to know what you don't know. Knowing brings great assurance. The children's classic song, "Jesus Loves Me," states "Jesus loves me, this I know for the Bible tells me so." God has given us His Word to help us to *know* and find assurance in that knowledge.

GETTING ACQUAINTED

Confucious (or Chuck) Says . . .

A recent best-seller bears the provocative title, *Everything I Need to Know I Learned in Kindergarten.* The author believes that cardinal truths are learned early and last a lifetime—truths such as "hold hands and stay together," "clean up your own mess," "don't be selfish." Over the course of our lifetime we have learned millions of truths. What's one truth that you would choose to pass on to the next generation?

Confucious is credited with wise sayings. For example, Confucious says: "He who sins against Heaven has nowhere left for prayer." In the same vein let's share a truth we've learned.

Now think of something you would like to learn. Is it information, a skill, insight? Write it here.

Let's find out what you know. Below list the members of your group. In the column to the right, list something you know about each individual.

Member	**What I Know**
_____	_____
_____	_____
_____	_____
_____	_____
_____	_____

GAINING INSIGHT

Scripture Study
Name the capitol of Illinois. 4 + 6 = ? When did you learn to tie your shoes? How persons learn has fascinated educators and psychologists for years. We are still unraveling the code that will help us teach and learn more effectively. We know that 50 percent of the development of general intel-

ligence occurs before a child is five; that by the time a baby is seven months, he can play with his own feet because hand-foot coordination has been learned; that conceptual thinking probably doesn't occur until the early teen years.

God has gifted us with the capacity to learn and we continue to pursue learning until we die. To be alive is to want to learn something new. As Christians we have been gifted with a whole Book of Truth to be learned. This Truth is more than just content to be understood and memorized. It is reality to be lived. Some people see the Bible as just a collection of stories, some of which are hard to understand. Romans 15:4 informs us that the Scriptures were written to teach us—to encourage us to hope.

Jesus was most often addressed in the Gospels as Rabbi. A Rabbi was a respected teacher. Jesus was constantly a Teacher. Whenever He encountered people, He informed, instructed, and enlarged their mental and spiritual boundaries. He was Truth personified. In fact, He entered the human race so that we might know and understand. He came that people might understand the true meaning of the Father's words; so that they might know the Father and His ways; so that they might live according to His guidelines and know His teaching. His small group was continually learning from their Teacher.

Probably one of the most memorable collections of curriculum taught by Jesus is what we today call the *Sermon on the Mount.* Here, Jesus teaches us God's standards for living a godly life. As you read the passages below, take sermon notes, writing down what you learn as you read each paragraph.

[19]**"Do not store up for yourselves treasures on earth, where moth and rust destroy, and where thieves break in and steal.** [20]**But store up for yourselves treasures in heaven, where moth and rust do not destroy, and where thieves do not break in and steal.** [21]**For where your treasure is, there your heart will be also.**

[22]**"The eye is the lamp of the body. If your eyes are good, your whole body will be full of light.** [23]**But if your eyes are**

bad, your whole body will be full of darkness. If then the light within you is darkness, how great is that darkness!

24"No one can serve two masters. Either he will hate the one and love the other, or he will be devoted to the one and despise the other. You cannot serve both God and Money."

Matthew 6:19-24

What does Jesus teach in the following contrasts? Write the principle in your own words.

❏ Two Kinds of Treasures:

❏ Two Kinds of Eyes:

❏ Two Kinds of Masters:

What is one meaning this has for your life?

25"Therefore I tell you, do not worry about your life, what you will eat or drink; or about your body, what you will wear. Is not life more important than clothes? 26Look at the birds of the air; they do not sow or reap or store away in barns, and yet your heavenly Father feeds them. Are you not much more valuable than they? 27Who of you by worrying can add a single hour to his life?

28"And why do you worry about clothes? See how the lilies of the field grow. They do not labor or spin. 29Yet I tell you that not even Solomon in all his splendor was dressed like one of these. 30If that is how God clothes the grass of the field, which is here today and tomorrow is thrown into the fire, will He not much more clothe you, O you of little faith? 31So do not worry, saying, 'What shall we eat?' or 'What shall we drink?' or 'What shall we wear?' 32For the pagans run after all these things, and your heavenly Father knows that you need them. 33But seek first His kingdom and His

42

righteousness, and all these things will be given to you as well. ³⁴Therefore do not worry about tomorrow, for tomorrow will worry about itself. Each day has enough trouble of its own."

Matthew 6:25-34

What does Jesus teach about worry?

What kind of person is Jesus seeking to develop by teaching this?

What is an area in your life where a promise from this passage could make a difference? How would that show?

¹"Do not judge, or you too will be judged. ²For in the same way you judge others, you will be judged, and with the measure you use, it will be measured to you.

³"Why do you look at the speck of sawdust in your brother's eye and pay no attention to the plank in your own eye? ⁴How can you say to your brother, 'Let me take the speck out of your eye,' when all the time there is a plank in your own eye? ⁵You hypocrite, first take the plank out of your own eye, and then you will see clearly to remove the speck from your brother's eye."

Matthew 7:1-5

What is Jesus calling us to be in this passage?

Why is this a good rule for healthy living?

⁷"Ask and it will be given to you; seek and you will find; knock and the door will be opened to you. ⁸For everyone who asks receives; he who seeks finds; and to him who knocks, the door will be opened.

⁹"Which of you, if his son asks for bread, will give him a stone? ¹⁰Or if he asks for a fish, will give him a snake? ¹¹If

you, then, though you are evil, know how to give good gifts to your children, how much more will your Father in heaven give good gifts to those who ask Him! ¹²So in everything, do to others what you would have them do to you, for this sums up the Law and the Prophets."

Matthew 7:7-12

What information do you pick up from this passage?

What teaching in this section encourages you?

If people had been taking notes on Jesus' lectures they could have gone home with their notebooks filled. They could have spent days discussing the meanings of His profound truths. The Pharisees did just that. They studied and stored the Scriptures, but were condemned by Jesus. Sometimes the closing words of a professor tell you how you will be tested on the content taught. Jesus was apparently doing just that at the end of this passage.

²⁴"Therefore everyone who hears these words of Mine and puts them into practice is like a wise man who built his house on the rock. ²⁵The rain came down, the streams rose, and the winds blew and beat against that house; yet it did not fall, because it had its foundation on the rock. ²⁶But everyone who hears these words of Mine and does not put them into practice is like a foolish man who built his house on sand. ²⁷The rain came down, the streams rose, and the winds blew and beat against that house, and it fell with a great crash."

Matthew 7:24-27

What is the place of Scripture according to these verses?

GROWING BY DOING

Being Wise In Our Individual Lives
What do you learn about knowing and doing in Matthew 7:24-27?

What's one thing you know that you can do this day as a result of obeying the insights you have learned from the Sermon on the Mount?

Share with your group how you plan to do that. How can they encourage you to follow through this next week?

GOING THE SECOND MILE

Accountability Checkup
Tell someone something you learned and are going to put into practice. Ask him or her to hold you accountable by a certain time period.

FIVE

Changes

GroupSpeak: *"I don't know if I would have grown as much this past year if it weren't for my small group. They gave me the courage to risk changing how I feel about myself and supplied the support and accountability I needed to follow through. Someone once said, 'You are more likely to change in a group than you are by yourself,' and I certainly agree."*

I'm Growing

Growth is a fascinating thing. Sometimes it happens so slowly that we seem to be standing still. Do you recall having to wait until you were big enough to "reach the pedals," or how you stood on tiptoe to be tall enough for your head to come up to the line so you could ride the bumper cars at the amusement park? Other times, growth is almost visible as many a mother laments, looking at high-water pants and shirts outgrown in a year. Birthdays remind us that change is relentless.

GETTING ACQUAINTED

I Usta Think

Children are often aware of the vast changes in their thinking about the world and how it operates as they grow older. One child admitted, "I usta think that when it thundered God was

47

throwing bowling balls." Another confessed, "I usta think that God was an old man with a long white beard who sat up on a cloud watching us."

In what ways have you seen your thinking change over the years?

What is a change you feel good about in your life?

Suppose someone met you after a six months' absence and exclaimed, "My, how you've grown!" To what would they be referring?

Can you think of ways you have grown recently in the following areas?

❑ Mentally

❑ Relationally

❑ Skillwise

❑ Personally

What kinds of things prompt growth in you? Can you discover any patterns?

 ## GAINING INSIGHT

Scripture Study
In the spiritual realm we also grow—sometimes by small steps hardly noticeable and at other times by giant leaps

forward. Looking back, we can often see evidences of growth in our understanding and changes in our attitudes and behaviors.

As you look back, can you think of a time when it was evident that you grew spiritually? What evidences did you notice? What prompted growth at this time?

Scripture indicates that Jesus expected His small group (The Twelve) to grow in understanding of who He was, resulting in increasing faith. Toward the end of their small group time, Jesus talked about going back to the Father. Let's examine the following passages of Scripture to discover what was expected to prompt growth in each of these instances.

⁸Philip said, "Lord, show us the Father and that will be enough for us." ⁹Jesus answered: "Don't you know Me, Philip, even after I have been among you such a long time? Anyone who has seen Me has seen the Father. How can you say, 'Show us the Father'?"

John 14:8-9

What prompted growth in this situation?

In John 10, Jesus tells the Jews that miracles are opportunities for growth in learning. Read John 10:36-38.

³⁶"What about the One whom the Father set apart as His very own and sent into the world? Why then do you accuse Me of blasphemy because I said, 'I am God's Son'? ³⁷Do not believe me unless I do what My Father does. ³⁸But if I do it, even though you do not believe Me, believe the miracles, that you may know and understand that the Father is in Me, and I in the Father."

John 10:36-38

What prompted growth in this situation?

Let's look at two happenings which could have caused growth in the disciples. Here's the setting.

³⁰The apostles gathered around Jesus and reported to Him all they had done and taught. ³¹Then, because so many people were coming and going that they did not even have a chance to eat, He said to them, "Come with Me by yourselves to a quiet place and get some rest."

³²So they went away by themselves in a boat to a solitary place. ³³But many who saw them leaving recognized them and ran on foot from all the towns and got there ahead of them. ³⁴When Jesus landed and saw a large crowd, He had compassion on them, because they were like sheep without a shepherd. So he began teaching them many things.

³⁵By this time it was late in the day, so His disciples came to Him. "This is a remote place," they said, "and it's already very late. ³⁶Send the people away so they can go to the surrounding countryside and villages and buy themselves something to eat." ³⁷But He answered, "You give them something to eat." They said to Him, "That would take eight months of a man's wages! Are we to go and spend that much on bread and give it to them to eat?" ³⁸"How many loaves do you have?" He asked. "Go and see." When they found out, they said, "Five—and two fish."

³⁹Then Jesus directed them to have all the people sit down in groups on the green grass. ⁴⁰So they sat down in groups of hundreds and fifties. ⁴¹Taking the five loaves and the two fish and looking up to heaven, He gave thanks and broke the loaves. Then He gave them to His disciples to set before the people. He also divided the two fish among them all. ⁴²They all ate and were satisfied, ⁴³and the disciples picked up twelve basketfuls of broken pieces of bread and fish. ⁴⁴The number of the men who had eaten was five thousand.

Mark 6:30-44

What prompted growth in this situation?

50

Next comes the "test" on Jesus' material.

⁴⁵Immediately Jesus made His disciples get into the boat and go on ahead of Him to Bethsaida, while He dismissed the crowd. ⁴⁶After leaving them, He went up on a mountainside to pray.

⁴⁷When evening came, the boat was in the middle of the lake, and he was alone on land. ⁴⁸He saw the disciples straining at the oars, because the wind was against them. About the fourth watch of the night He went out to them, walking on the lake. He was about to pass by them, ⁴⁹but when they saw Him walking on the lake, they thought He was a ghost. They cried out, ⁵⁰because they all saw Him and were terrified. Immediately He spoke to them and said, "Take courage! It is I. Don't be afraid."

⁵¹Then He climbed into the boat with them, and the wind died down. They were completely amazed, ⁵²for they had not understood about the loaves; their hearts were hardened.

Mark 6:45-52

What prompted growth in this situation?

This event was a test of what Jesus had sought to teach the disciples when He fed the 5,000. What did He want them to recognize about Himself?

Now let's examine another opportunity for the disciples to grow.

¹During those days another large crowd gathered. Since they had nothing to eat, Jesus called His disciples to Him and said, ²"I have compassion for these people; they have already been with Me three days and have nothing to eat. ³If I send them home hungry, they will collapse on the way, because some of them have come a long distance."

51

⁴His disciples answered, "But where in this remote place can anyone get enough bread to feed them?" ⁵"How many loaves do you have?" Jesus asked. "Seven," they replied.

⁶He told the crowd to sit down on the ground. When He had taken the seven loaves and given thanks, He broke them and gave them to His disciples to set before the people, and they did so. ⁷They had a few small fish as well; He gave thanks for them also and told the disciples to distribute them. ⁸The people ate and were satisfied. Afterward the disciples picked up seven basketfuls of broken pieces that were left over. ⁹About four thousand men were present. And having sent them away, ¹⁰He got into the boat with His disciples and went to the region of Dalmanutha.

Mark 8:1-10

What prompted growth in this situation?

Let's look at the test following this occasion. Read Mark 8:14-21.

¹⁴The disciples had forgotten to bring bread, except for one loaf they had with them in the boat. ¹⁵"Be careful," Jesus warned them. "Watch out for the yeast of the Pharisees and that of Herod." ¹⁶They discussed this with one another and said, "It is because we have no bread." ¹⁷Aware of their discussion, Jesus asked them: "Why are you talking about having no bread? Do you still not see or understand? Are your hearts hardened? ¹⁸Do you have eyes but fail to see, and ears but fail to hear? And don't you remember? ¹⁹When I broke the five loaves for the five thousand, how many basketfuls of pieces did you pick up?"

"Twelve," they replied.

²⁰"And when I broke the seven loaves for the four thousand, how many basketfuls of pieces did you pick up?"

52

They answered, "Seven."

²¹He said to them, "Do you still not understand?"

Mark 8:14-21

Jesus warned the disciples about the infectious impact of the Pharisees and Herod who resisted the Truth.

What was the disciples' concern? (v. 16)

Why was it unbelievable to Jesus that they would struggle with this issue? (vv. 18-20)

Of what does Jesus accuse the disciples that prevents their growth in understanding? (vv. 17-18)

Describe an area in your life where you would like to grow.

GROWING BY DOING

Present Learning Opportunity
What are some present situations where God is teaching you about Himself? Are these lessons helping you to grow?

If you cannot yet see a learning opportunity in a situation, ask God to show you what He wants to reveal about Himself.

GOING THE SECOND MILE

Take Time To Give Thanks
Take time at each meal during the next week to thank God for one of the specific growth evidences mentioned by a group member.

53

SIX

Caring

GroupSpeak: *"I think it was in a group that I first experienced feeling really cared for. I found I could just be myself and they would accept me. I think it was one of the major developments in helping me come to know God and to feel comfortable with Him."*

Try It, You'll Like It
"When you care enough to send the very best," you send Hallmark. Or if you *really* care, you "reach out and touch someone," according to AT&T.

The popular show *Cheers* shows us that the place where everybody knows our name is the neighborhood bar. Singles' bars and personal ads have become vehicles where people unashamedly advertise their longing for care.

Jesus intends for His followers to care for one another. Knowing our need to be cared for, He sent the Spirit to serve as "another Comforter" after He had gone. He also built His disciples into a community—a caring community that would provide the love and nurture needed to survive in a non-caring world; a community that would treat the servants as it had treated the Lord.

55

GETTING ACQUAINTED

Care Packages

A desire for care is built into us as persons. We all want somebody to say, "I care." Share your answers to the following questions with the group.

When you think of "care-givers" in your life, who comes to mind?

When was a time when you really felt cared for? What did the other person do?

What kinds of care packages communicate "I care" to you?

☐ Cards and notes?
☐ Hugs and touching?
☐ Gifts?
☐ Spending time with you?
☐ Sharing your projects and concerns?
☐ Phone calls?
☐ Listening?
☐ Praying?
☐ Other?

Who Cares!

Thousands of years ago one brother posed a question that has been repeated in various forms through ages of history. "Am I my brother's keeper?" (Genesis 4:9) Although much has changed in our society since Cain uttered those provocative words, we still ponder that question today: "For whom am I responsible to care?" We have become content to pick up a Hallmark card and send it as expression of our care and feel that our duty is done. But the impersonalness of our world magnifies our loneliness. People today are longing for someone to care.

What evidences of lack of caring have come to your awareness? How have we become an impersonal society?

56

This current scenario of impersonal, non-caring, distancing ourselves from others did not occur overnight. It has its roots in many strands of values and ways of thinking.

What are some understandable reasons for our not finding it necessary to feel with and for others if we want to survive in our present world?

Look at the reasons people give for *not* caring. Which of these seem true in your life? Add your list of excuses to those below.

❑ Takes too much energy and time
❑ Afraid to care and trust
❑ Too many people to care for
❑ Don't want to create dependency or be misunderstood
❑ Other:

How does all this translate into the church? Of all places, believers long to find in the church community a place of belonging and care.

We in this group are no different. Probably a major reason why you are here is your desire to find a relationship where you can care and be cared for. But small groups don't automatically become caring communities just because Christians with good intentions gather together. The same hindrances to caring experienced by society are present in Christian communities.

Have any of the following thoughts gone through your mind since our group has begun meeting?

❑ I don't know if I want to generate the emotional energy it requires to be caring.

❑ I wonder if caring will undermine my own agendas and desires to do what I want. Will I feel trapped?

❏ Can I trust these people? Can I be vulnerable? Will they really care? Will they understand me?

❏ Will they think I am inadequate as a person if I need their care?

❏ Are these people a priority in my life? What if I just naturally don't care to go any deeper in my caring? Can I admit that without them feeling rejected?

❏ What if I don't know how to care? What if I'm so preoccupied with my own issues that I can't care?

These feelings are present in any group. We long to be cared for, but we feel hesitant to be open. We want to be caring because we know Jesus would care, but we are torn by other concerns and values that raise warning flags when we think of giving care to another.

GAINING INSIGHT

Scripture Study

Jesus sought to build a caring community among His disciples. The fact that He succeeded is verified by the model that is perpetuated in the early chapters of the Acts. The early Church became a reflection of the disciples' community. They obeyed His command, "Go and make disciples ... teaching them to obey everything I have commanded you" (Matthew 28:19-20).

What factors would have made it difficult for the disciples to become a group that cared for each other?

Because the disciples were constantly confronted with needy persons, they could have easily overlooked one another's needs. But the disciples had a Master who exhibited great care for them. Let's look at two glimpses into the caring dilemma experienced by the disciples. The first involves our natural desire to care for ourselves even when it means not caring about others.

35Then James and John, the sons of Zebedee, came to Him. "Teacher," they said, "we want You to do for us whatever we ask."

36"What do you want Me to do for you?" he asked.

37They replied, "Let one of us sit at Your right and the other at Your left in Your glory."

38"You don't know what you are asking," Jesus said. "Can you drink the cup I drink or be baptized with the baptism I am baptized with?"

39"We can," they answered.

Jesus said to them, "You will drink the cup I drink and be baptized with the baptism I am baptized with, 40but to sit at My right or left is not for Me to grant. These places belong to those for whom they have been prepared."

41When the ten heard about this, they became indignant with James and John. 42Jesus called them together and said, "You know that those who are regarded as rulers of the Gentiles lord it over them, and their high officials exercise authority over them. 43Not so with you. Instead, whoever wants to become great among you must be your servant, 44and whoever wants to be first must be slave of all. 45For even the Son of Man did not come to be served, but to serve, and to give His life as a ransom for many."

Mark 10:35-45

How do you see Jesus showing care for James and John? How does He care for the other disciples?

What do you think the phrase "they became indignant with James and John" means? (v. 41)

How did Jesus indicate that this was a caring issue for the whole group? Why is it caring to face group issues head on?

How is a desire for greatness among others an uncaring attitude? (v. 43)

How did Jesus describe the way Gentiles built relationships? How are Jesus' followers to be different?

What principles for nurturing care among believers would you list from this incident?

An interesting postscript is that never again among the disciples is there recorded a "me-first" situation. Rather, the Book of Acts describes what appears to be support of the giftedness of various individuals. The eleven stood up with Peter as he delivered his Pentecost address (Acts 2:14). They harmoniously worked out the friction of service in Acts 6.

Now, let's look at a second caring dilemma experienced by the disciples. Situation number two is found in John 13:2-17.

²The evening meal was being served, and the devil had already prompted Judas Iscariot, son of Simon, to betray Jesus. ³Jesus knew that the Father had put all things under His power, and that He had come from God and was returning to God; so He got up from the meal, took off His outer clothing, and wrapped a towel around His waist. ⁵After that, he poured water into a basin and began to wash His disciples' feet, drying them with the towel that was wrapped around Him.

⁶He came to Simon Peter, who said to Him, "Lord, are You going to wash my feet?"

⁷Jesus replied, "You do not realize now what I am doing, but later you will understand."

⁸"No," said Peter, "You shall never wash my feet."

Jesus answered, "Unless I wash you, you have no part with Me."

⁹"Then, Lord," Simon Peter replied, "not just my feet but my hands and my head as well!"

¹⁰Jesus answered, "A person who has had a bath needs only to wash his feet; his whole body is clean. And you are clean, though not every one of you." ¹¹For He knew who was going to betray Him, and that was why He said not every one was clean.

¹²When He had finished washing their feet, He put on His clothes and returned to His place. "Do you understand what I have done for you?" He asked them. ¹³"You call Me 'Teacher' and 'Lord,' and rightly so, for that is what I am. ¹⁴Now that I, your Lord and Teacher, have washed your feet, you also should wash one another's feet. ¹⁵I have set you an example that you should do as I have done for you. ¹⁶I tell you the truth, no servant is greater than his master, nor is a messenger greater than the one who sent him. ¹⁷Now that you know these things, you will be blessed if you do them."

John 13:2-17

If you could come up with a Hallmark-type slogan for Jesus' kind of caring as exhibited here, what would it be?

In what ways do you see Jesus demonstrating care here?

Jesus wants to make sure the disciples catch His message, so in verse 12 He inquires regarding their insight. Notice how personal His question is: "Do you understand what I have done for you?" An awareness of what caring does for us personally, prompts us to realize the importance of doing this for others. In 2 Corinthians 1:4, Paul notes that God comforts us, "so that we can comfort those in any trouble with the comfort we ourselves have received from God."

How does Jesus call the disciples to henceforth care for one another in John 13?

What is meant by "you also should wash one another's feet"? What opportunities do we have to care for each other?

What principles for caregiving are found in John 13?

 ## GROWING BY DOING

Caring Among Us
The passage in John 13 ends with, "Now that you know these things, you will be blessed if you do them" (v. 17). Take a few minutes to think about how these principles can be worked out as practical ways of caring in our group.

How can we motivate each other to care about each other?

What hinders caring in our group?

Complete this sentence: One way I'd like to be cared for in our group is . . .

GOING THE SECOND MILE

Care Card

Let your "I Care" card or sticker remind you to follow up on your commitment to your Care Buddy.

SEVEN

Service

GroupSpeak: *"It was in a small group that I first recognized I had the gift of encouragement. When people shared how I had ministered to them, I began to realize that God was doing something through me that I hadn't been conscious of."*

Made For The Body

As a world watched in horror the space shuttle Challenger exploded in flight, plummeting its occupants to the ocean floor, and leaving the onlookers aghast with disbelief. The pain of this awful experience was not eased by subsequent investigation of its cause. The problem? A small O-ring seal had ceased to perform its function. A technical marvel, costing millions of dollars, and eight lives were destroyed.

In a graphic way, this disaster portrays the importance of every part contributing for the good of a larger goal. The most sophisticated technological equipment on board was not of more importance than that vital O-ring.

The Word of God puts it this way, "There are many parts, but one body. The eye cannot say to the hand, 'I don't need you!' And the head cannot say to the feet, 'I don't need you!' " (1 Corinthians 12:20-21) Or, "From him [Christ] the whole body, joined and held together by every supporting ligament, grows and builds itself up in love, *as each part does its work*" (Ephesians 4:16).

The common good of building up the body and nurturing it in unity is the purpose for which God has given us ministry gifts (1 Corinthians 12:7). We are responsible for serving one another with our God-given abilities (Romans 12:4-5).

GETTING ACQUAINTED

What Is Your Opinion?
When you hear the term "spiritual gifts," what comes to mind?

What do you think about spiritual gifts?

Agree	Disagree	
____	____	1. The presence or absence of spiritual gifts is a good measurement of a Christian's spirituality.
____	____	2. Gifts are given by God's Spirit; people have nothing to do with them.
____	____	3. A gift is a talent that has been dedicated to God.
____	____	4. God may withdraw as well as give gifts because He is sovereign.
____	____	5. Once given, gifts do not change.

_____   _____   6. If you don't use a gift, it will be withdrawn.

_____   _____   7. Each person must accept personal responsibility for the discovery, development, and use of his or her spiritual gift.

_____   _____   8. Gifts are to unify the body of Christ and to help us reach the world for Christ.

_____   _____   9. Knowing what your gift is will not be as important as walking in the Spirit.

_____   _____   10. Some Christians have no spiritual gift and some continually receive more.

Are there any more statements that you would add to the above list?

 ## GAINING INSIGHT

Let's Build Something
Suppose as a group we decided to build a cabin or outfit a nursery.

Who in our group would you expect to:

❏ head up the project

❏ figure out how to get a loan

❏ estimate the supplies needed

❏ have all the right tools

❏ design a blueprint

❏ hang wallpaper

❏ design curtains

❏ choose decorative pieces for the interior

People would naturally gravitate to leading us in certain responsibilities, but no one would be more valuable than another. Every job needs to be done. What some seem to do with ease is done with more difficulty by others.

What kinds of assumptions could sidetrack the project?

What thoughts could prompt action (or lack of action) that could prevent the project from happening?

These same kinds of thoughts enable or hinder a small group from being all it could be. While we may or may not have the expertise to construct a cabin using members of our group, God has placed in each of us everything we need to meet His expectations for our small group. In fact, as we have spent these weeks together, one of the most important things we have been doing is developing an awareness of the special ways each one of us contributes to the building up of our group.

Husbands and wives who give each other gifts so the giver can benefit from the availability of the gift are often the brunt of jokes. He gets her a new table saw for their anniversary so he can use it in his workshop to make her some new shelves. She gets him a new vacuum cleaner so she can clean his work area.

But receiving special giftedness and inclinations from God is like receiving a large sum of money which you must spend on another if you choose to spend it. Special abilities are not given to be squandered on the individual, but rather to be lavished on the body of Christ. The joy comes in giving away what you have that will benefit other believers. Your contribution causes the whole body of Christ to be enriched and strengthened.

Scripture Study

An example of gifts being used for the building of the body of Christ is found in Acts 6.

¹In those days when the number of disciples was increasing, the Grecian Jews among them complained against the Hebraic Jews because their widows were being overlooked in the daily distribution of food. ²So the Twelve gathered all the disciples together and said, "It would not be right for us to neglect the ministry of the word of God in order to wait on tables. ³Brothers, choose seven men from among you who are known to be full of the Spirit and wisdom. We will turn this responsibility over to them ⁴and will give our attention to prayer and the ministry of the word."

⁵This proposal pleased the whole group. They chose Stephen, a man full of faith and of the Holy Spirit; also Philip, Procorus, Nicanor, Timon, Parmenas, and Nicolas from Antioch, a convert to Judaism. ⁶They presented these men to the apostles, who prayed and laid their hands on them.

⁷So the word of God spread. The number of disciples in Jerusalem increased rapidly, and a large number of priests became obedient to the faith.

⁸Now Stephen, a man full of God's grace and power, did great wonders and miraculous signs among the people.

Acts 6:1-8

In this situation what need arose in the disciples' group that forced them to call on others for help?

How would you describe the group function that took place in this passage?

What do the *when,* the *who,* and the *what* in Acts 6:1 add to this situation?

69

❏ *When* — "When the number of disciples was increasing." How would this contribute to the problem?

❏ *Who* — "Grecian Jews . . . against the Hebraic Jews." What added tension does this suggest?

❏ *What* — "Their widows were being overlooked in the daily distribution of food." Why would this be such a dynamic issue?

In the face of these complaints, what assessment did the disciples make?

What solution did they come up with?

What were the qualities needed by a potential candidate to be chosen for service by the disciples?

What gift of service did the Twelve offer to the group?

What did the disciples observe in Stephen that caused them to choose him?

What further role did the Twelve have in regard to these chosen men?

Why did they pray for and lay hands on those who would distribute food to hungry widows?

What does this tell you about the role these people had as they contributed their abilities to the group?

What was the result of everyone contributing what was given to him or her for the good of all?

How does the response in Acts 6 illustrate the body concept found in 1 Corinthians 12:7 and Ephesians 4:16?

Read 1 Corinthians 12:12-21, 24b-27 which compares Christians to a body.

¹²The body is a unit, though it is made up of many parts; and though all its parts are many, they form one body. So it is with Christ. ¹³For we were all baptized by one Spirit into one body—whether Jews or Greeks, slave or free—and we were all given the one Spirit to drink.

¹⁴Now the body is not made up of one part but of many. ¹⁵If the foot should say, "Because I am not a hand, I do not belong to the body," it would not for that reason cease to be part of the body. ¹⁶And if the ear should say, "Because I am not an eye, I do not belong to the body," it would not for that reason cease to be part of the body. ¹⁷If the whole body were an eye, where would the sense of hearing be? If the whole body were an ear, where would the sense of smell be? ¹⁸But in fact God has arranged the parts in the body, every one of them, just as He wanted them to be. ¹⁹If they were all one part, where would the body be? ²⁰As it is, there are many parts, but one body.

²¹**The eye cannot say to the hand, "I don't need you!" And the head cannot say to the feet, "I don't need you!"**

²⁴**But God has combined the members of the body and has given greater honor to the parts that lacked it,** ²⁵**so that there should be no division in the body, but that its parts should have equal concern for each other.** ²⁶**If one part suffers, every part suffers with it; if one part is honored, every part rejoices with it.**

²⁷**Now you are the body of Christ, and each one of you is a part of it.**

1 Corinthians 12:12-21, 24b-27

What are two main principles you find in the passage?

Main Idea #1

Main Idea #2

How do you see these principles operating in our small group?

 ## GROWING BY DOING

Who's Who

Small groups are hothouses for nurturing and recognizing abilities that God has given people for the good of all. It is often in a small group setting that a person realizes from the feedback from others that he or she is especially prepared to help the rest of the body of Christ in a particular area. Let's look at the following phrases and identify who in our group seems to be better at this aspect than others. If you wish to tie in the described roles with the biblical spiritual gifts, they are identified in parentheses.

1. _____ seems particularly good in counseling people who need help with personal problems (exhortation).

2. _____ appears to enjoy studying in order to teach us something new (teaching).

3. _____ feels more at ease helping another person than teaching, assuming leadership, etc. (ministry).

4. _____ seems to be fairly effective in communicating God's Word to groups of believers (prophecy).

5. _____ is able to uncover fresh insights from God's Word with little help from other sources (prophecy).

6. _____ shows ability in communicating a truth that someone else has taught him or her (teaching).

7. _____ enjoys providing resources to individuals or groups in need (giving).

8. _____ is often found encouraging individuals, helping them to go on in their walk with the Lord (exhortation).

9. _____ frequently finds himself or herself in the place of leading and feels at ease being in that position (leadership).

10. _____ is particularly good in motivating our group to get a task done (leadership).

11. _____ seems effective in guiding us in decisions and activities, shepherding us (leadership).

12. _____ has a warm heart toward people and likes to come alongside them, often encouraging growth through giving personal counsel (exhortation).

13. _____ tries to do something for persons who are in distress (mercy).

14. _____ enjoys pitching in to help on a task that needs to be done (ministry).

15. _____ responds to those who are suffering and seeks to do something (mercy).

16. _____ receives a special delight from giving something to another (giving).

17. _____ receives comments from others on how helpful or clear his or her teaching is (teaching).

18. _____ shows godly wisdom in communication that seems to build up believers (prophecy).

19. _____ is often called upon by others because he/she shows genuine enjoyment in assisting another (ministry).

20. _____ is usually concerned about persons who need food, clothing, or other types of aid (giving).

21. _____ is usually sensitive to hurting individuals, wanting to comfort the one who has been embarrassed or humiliated (mercy).

22. _____ would be one of the first to come to our aid if one of us fell and hurt himself or herself (mercy).

23. _____ frequently has individuals coming to him/her for assistance in solving some spiritual problem (exhortation).

24. _____ is looked to by us because he/she is fair, enjoyable to work with, and motivates others to get the job done (leadership).

25. _____ is often busy doing something for someone else, or volunteering whenever help is needed (ministry).

GOING THE SECOND MILE

Personal Checkup

What did you discover about yourself in the group time?

What did the group consider that you do best?

What's one way you could put your giftedness into action this week?

EIGHT

Celebration

GroupSpeak: *"It was the presence of Jesus that made our group what it was. Many times we sensed He was there."*

God With Us

Community is God's idea. He exists in community and is conscious of the interdependence that binds the Godhead together. The Father depends upon the Son to reveal who He is to humankind (John 17:6; 14:10). The Son reflects His focused dependence on the Father:

❑ "These words you hear are not My own; they belong to the Father who sent Me" (John 14:24).

❑ "I do nothing on My own but speak just what the Father has taught Me" (John 8:28).

❑ "By myself I can do nothing; I judge only as I hear" (John 5:30).

❑ "The Son can do nothing by Himself; He can do only what He sees His Father doing" (John 5:19).

In speaking of the Spirit, Jesus announced, "He will not speak on His own; He will speak only what He hears" (John 16:13). The Godhead itself lives in relational community.

The creation of Adam was called good, but his aloneness was pronounced not good by God Himself. Eve must be there for community. In the garden lifestyle, it was God who entered into community and built relationship with both Adam and Eve. Throughout the Old Testament, the Israelites found their identity in community. And the strongest form of punishment was banishment from that community. God declares Himself to be the God of Israel and to dwell among them.

Jesus built a community among the Twelve. In many ways this tiny community was reflective of the kingdom, for it was a kingdom of relationships that bridged across class lines and social roles. The Twelve's allegiance to Him as Lord bound them together with bonds that endured the crucifixion and persecution. The Book of Acts demonstrates God at work, creating pockets of supportive, caring fellowships that confounded the individualistic pagan world.

God values community development. In a special way, He graces those occasions of coming together with His very own presence. He is between believers, among His family, within small groups focused on Him, whether they be 2 or 3 or 23. He is a God who is with His people—not a God who distances Himself from us.

GETTING ACQUAINTED

It Pays To Advertise

In the space below, write an advertisement for your group, incorporating all the plus items of your group members. How would you sell another person on the value of your group? What elements would appeal?

78

What seems most important in your description? What events stand out? What impressed you so much that it became a part of your description?

Memorable Moments
Spend some time walking down memory lane.

How has our group attendance been?

Who has been here every single time?

Did our group seem different when one person was missing?

Where two or three persons come together in His name, Jesus promises to be there. What is unique about a Christian small group where Jesus is present?

GAINING INSIGHT

Scripture Study
Small groups are everywhere today. The February 5, 1990 issue of *Newsweek* ran a cover story on the range of support groups and claimed that there are 500,000 groups estimated in existence today with 15 million Americans in attendance. Their researchers identified support groups for everything from abused wives of doctors to zoologists who love too much.

For many of us this has become a support group. But this is a *Christian* small group. What do you think makes a group *Christian?* What is different about a Christian small group?

God thought of community long before there were any small groups. Jesus enhanced the value of such interpersonal relationships by claiming, "Where two or three come together in My name, there am I with them" (Matthew 18:20).

When Jesus is present in a small group, that group changes. Let's look at two incidents which demonstrate this.

NARRATOR: [13]Now that same day two of them were going to a village called Emmaus, about seven miles from Jerusalem. [14]They were talking with each other about everything that had happened. [15]As they talked and discussed these things with each other, Jesus Himself came up and walked along with them; [16]but they were kept from recognizing Him. [17]He asked them,

JESUS: "What are you discussing together as you walk along?"

NARRATOR: They stood still, their faces downcast. [18]One of them, named Cleopas, asked Him,

CLEOPAS: "Are You only a visitor to Jerusalem and do not know the things that have happened there in these days?"

JESUS: [19]"What things?"

NARRATOR: He asked.

CLEOPAS: "About Jesus of Nazareth. He was a prophet, powerful in word and deed before God and all the people. [20]The chief priests and our rulers handed Him over to be sentenced to death, and they crucified Him; [21]but we had hoped that He was one who was going to redeem Israel. And what is more, it is the third day since all this took place. [22]In addition, some of our women amazed us. They went to the tomb early this morning [23]but didn't find His body. They came and told us that they had seen a vision of angels, who said He was alive. [24]Then some of our companions went to the tomb and found it just

80

as the women had said, but Him they did not see."

NARRATOR: ²⁵He said to them,

JESUS: "How foolish you are, and how slow of heart to believe all that the prophets have spoken! ²⁶Did not the Christ have to suffer these things and then enter His glory?"

NARRATOR: And beginning with Moses and all the Prophets, he explained to them what was said in all the Scriptures concerning Himself. ²⁸As they approached the village to which they were going, Jesus acted as if He were going farther. ²⁹But they urged Him strongly,

CLEOPAS: "Stay with us, for it is nearly evening; the day is almost over."

NARRATOR: So He went in to stay with them. ³⁰When He was at the table with them, He took bread, gave thanks, broke it and began to give it to them. ³¹Then their eyes were opened and they recognized Him, and He disappeared from their sight. ³²They asked each other,

CLEOPAS: "Were not our hearts burning within us while He talked with us on the road and opened the Scriptures to us?"

NARRATOR: ³³They got up and returned at once to Jerusalem. There they found the Eleven and those with them assembled together ³⁴and saying,

ELEVEN: "It is true! The Lord has risen and has appeared to Simon."

NARRATOR: ³⁵Then the two told what had happened on the way, and how Jesus was recognized by them when He broke the bread.

Luke 24:13-35

How did Jesus' presence change the attitude of the group?

Can you suggest any way that you have seen an attitude change because the presence of Jesus was felt in the life of one of our members or in our group?

How did Jesus seek to verify who He was? What did He do to help them believe Him? Why do you think He chose to do these things?

What kinds of things have helped you to believe in Him with greater commitment because of being in this group?

What was Jesus' role with the Scriptures? Why was this so important?

In what way or ways has the Spirit of Jesus helped you understand the Scriptures? What is something you have learned?

What emotions do you see expressed in this group?

What were the results or outcomes of Jesus being with the people in this passage? How did He change them? What did they become?

Now let's look at a second incident where Jesus' presence changed a group.

NARRATOR: ³⁶While they were still talking about this, Jesus Himself stood among them and said to them,

JESUS: "Peace be with you."

NARRATOR: ³⁷They were startled and frightened, thinking they saw a ghost. ³⁸He said to them,

JESUS: "Why are you troubled, and why do doubts rise in your minds? ³⁹Look at My hands and My feet. It is I myself! Touch Me and see; a ghost does not have flesh and bones, as you see I have."

NARRATOR: ⁴⁰When He had said this, He showed them His hands and feet. ⁴¹And while they still did not believe it because of joy and amazement, He asked them,

JESUS: "Do you have anything here to eat?"

NARRATOR: ⁴²They gave Him a piece of broiled fish, ⁴³and He took it and ate it in their presence. ⁴⁴He said to them,

JESUS: "This is what I told you while I was still with you: Everything must be fulfilled that is written about Me in the Law of Moses, the Prophets and the Psalms."

NARRATOR: ⁴⁵Then He opened their minds so they could understand the Scriptures. ⁴⁶He told them,

JESUS: "This is what is written: The Christ will suffer and rise from the dead on the third day, ⁴⁷and repentance and forgiveness of sins will be preached in His name to all nations, beginning at Jerusalem. ⁴⁸You are witnesses of these things. ⁴⁹I am going to send you what My Father has promised; but stay in the city until you

have been clothed with power from on high."
Luke 24:36-49

How did Jesus' presence change the attitude of the group?

Can you suggest any way that you have seen an attitude change because the presence of Jesus was felt in the life of one of our members or in our group?

How did Jesus seek to verify who He was? What did He do to help them believe Him? Why do you think He chose to do these things?

What kinds of things have helped you to believe in Him with greater commitment because of being in this group?

What was Jesus' role with the Scriptures? Why was this so important?

In what way or ways has the Spirit of Jesus helped you understand the Scriptures? What is something you have learned?

What emotions do you see expressed in this group?

What were the results or outcomes of Jesus being with the people in this passage? How did He change them? What did they become?

GROWING BY DOING

My Testimony

The Scripture we have just studied indicates that being in a group where Jesus is present gives persons in the group something to share. The witnesses in Luke 24 shared what they had experienced. They talked about who Jesus was and what He had done. Because Jesus has been present in our group, we can do that also.

Having been in this group where the presence of Jesus has been felt, of what could you give witness?

What do you know of Him from this group?

How have people in this group been an instrument of Jesus in your life?

Thank-You God

What about your group would you include in a thank-You note to God? What specific thanksgivings do you have?

Dear God,

As I think about the people with whom I've spent this group experience, I am particularly thankful for

GOING THE SECOND MILE

Share Some Pleasant Words

After this last session, why not call someone in the group and share with him or her something about the group that continues to impress you as being a good gift from God. Maybe it is something someone said or did during the last session. Maybe it is a comment remembered from earlier times. Maybe it is an attitude that helped color the group in a positive way for you. As Proverbs says, "Pleasant words are a honeycomb, sweet to the soul and healing to the bones" (Proverbs 16:24).

DEAR SMALL GROUP LEADER:

Picture Yourself As A Leader.

List some words that describe what would excite you or scare you as a leader of your small group.

A Leader Is Not . . .
- ❑ a person with all the answers.
- ❑ responsible for everyone having a good time.
- ❑ someone who does all the talking.
- ❑ likely to do everything perfectly.

A Leader Is . . .
- ❑ someone who encourages and enables group members to discover insights and build relationships.
- ❑ a person who helps others meet their goals, enabling the group to fulfill its purpose.
- ❑ a protector to keep members from being attacked or taken advantage of.
- ❑ the person who structures group time and plans ahead.
- ❑ the facilitator who stimulates relationships and participation by asking questions.
- ❑ an affirmer, encourager, challenger.

❑ enthusiastic about the small group, about God's Word, and about discovering and growing.

What Is Important To Small Group Members?
❑ A leader who cares about them.
❑ Building relationships with other members.
❑ Seeing themselves grow.
❑ Belonging and having a place in the group.
❑ Feeling safe while being challenged.
❑ Having their reasons for joining a group fulfilled.

What Do You Do . . .

If nobody talks—
❑ Wait—show the group members you expect them to answer.
❑ Rephrase a question—give them time to think.
❑ Divide into subgroups so all participate.

If somebody talks too much—
❑ Avoid eye contact with him or her.
❑ Sit beside the person next time. It will be harder for him or her to talk sitting by the leader.
❑ Suggest, "Let's hear from someone else."
❑ Interrupt with, "Great! Anybody else?"

If people don't know the Bible—
❑ Print out the passage in the same translation and hand it out to save time searching for a passage.
❑ Use the same Bible versions and give page numbers.
❑ Ask enablers to sit next to those who may need encouragement in sharing.
❑ Begin using this book to teach them how to study; affirm their efforts.

If you have a difficult individual—
❑ Take control to protect the group, but recognize that exploring differences can be a learning experience.
❑ Sit next to that person.
❑ To avoid getting sidetracked or to protect another group member, you may need to interrupt, saying, "Not all of us feel that way."
❑ Pray for that person before the group meeting.

ONE

Choices

"You have a choice" is a phrase that arouses our imagination, kindles our enthusiasm, and turns on our responsibility. People come to a group with different reasons. Some choose to come because of the leader, some because of another person in the group, some because of what they will gain — information, a sense of belonging and inclusion, friends, a realm for doing what they enjoy doing. Regardless of motives, each person must make a choice to come and participate in a community called small group. However, *community* as an attitude isn't automatic — it requires time and careful handling. Having a choice in what goes in a small group builds that sense of community.

"What I invest in becomes a part of me," or as the Master Teacher reported, "Where your treasure is, there your heart will be also" (Matthew 6:21). This session's emphasis on choices provides a way to get acquainted because a person's choices reveal who that person is. It also gives opportunity to display expectations and to make an investment in a small group so that right from the beginning it becomes "our" group.

As **Group Leader** of this small group experience, *you* have a choice as to which elements will best fit your group, your style of leadership, and your purposes. After you examine the

Session Objectives, select the activities under each heading with which to begin your community building. You have many choices.

SESSION OBJECTIVES

√ To become aware of why we are in this group and what we want to accomplish.
√ To set a pattern for sharing openly.
√ To find common threads among group members.
√ To identify with others in the group.

GETTING ACQUAINTED 20–30 minutes

Pocket Principle

1 The more time group members spend sharing their lives and experiences, the sooner will be their bonding into community. At the beginning of a group, spend a great deal of time allowing members to share.

If your group is not well acquainted, take time at least to get to know one another's names before beginning this session. If the group is strong in its relational bonds, the following exercises may help to strengthen the group.

Have a group member read aloud **You Have A Choice!** Then choose one of the following activities to help create a more comfortable, nonthreatening atmosphere for the first meeting of your small group.

Birds of a Feather

Identify three distinct areas of your room as **A, B,** and **C.** Ask group members to stand and to indicate their choice among three options (See page 14) by moving to the appropriate area that represents their preference. When each choice has been made, give assembled groups two minutes to share with one another why they made that particular choice. Encourage the group to discuss the questions under each choice.

Optional — Choices and Responsibilities
Ask each group member to think of a choice he or she made as a child or youth and then to share that choice and the resulting responsibility with other group members.

Optional — Pivotal Choices
Ask group members to share briefly a pivotal choice that they now see as a turning point in their lives. It could be a relationship that developed into a lifelong commitment, a career or schooling choice, a decision on where to live, or other opportunity embraced. If you have a large group (9 or more) you may want to divide into smaller groups so everyone can share in the time allotted. Give a 5 minute warning.

GAINING INSIGHT   20–25 minutes

Pocket Principle

2 The more group members talk about their understanding of how Scriptural principles relate to life, the more likely those principles are to transfer into their lives. Don't just tell; ask them to think and share.

Pocket Principle

3 The way a person participates during the first session with a group is likely to establish a pattern of participation. Help each group member respond at least once during this study to establish the habit of investing in the group.

Understanding Choices
Have group members turn to their neighbors and share at least five choices they've made today.

Scripture Study
Have group members take turns reading aloud this section as well as John 1:35-51. Then discuss the following questions.

❑ **What choices did Jesus' followers make in this passage?** (They chose to pursue Jesus, to spend time with

91

Him, to talk about Jesus, to bring people they cared about into Jesus' presence, to obey/act on what Jesus said.)

❑ **In what ways could the disciples' choices affect the rest of their lives?** (They were attracted to Jesus, and their enthusiasm about who He was affected everything they did. Two of John the Baptist's disciples made a choice that started them [and those related to them] on an exciting experience.)

Suggest that the group think about the following question as a group member reads aloud Mark 3:13-15, John 6:70a, John 15:16, 19 — **What impact do you think Jesus' words would have on the chosen disciples when they heard this?**

Discuss the following questions.

❑ **How do you feel when you are the chooser in a situation?** (Powerful, but responsible.)

❑ **How do you feel when you are the one chosen?** (Esteemed, valued, want to please the one who chose you.)

GROWING BY DOING   15–20 minutes
Thanking The Chooser
As the group prays, make sure that each member is prayed for either by others in the group or by you as the leader. You may want to ask group members to divide into pairs to pray specifically for one another.

Encourage each person to share the expectations or motivations that caused him or her to want to be in this small group. It is important to know group members' agendas. After each person shares his or her reasons for wanting to be a part of the group, summarize what has been expressed.

GOING THE SECOND MILE   5 minutes
Group Checkup
Challenge the group to spend some time during the next few

days thinking about the choices they made in this first session. They can complete the **Going the Second Mile** section on their own. However, encourage group members to share suggestions about ways to make the group what they desire it to be. Encourage them also to make contact with one other person before the next session.

GROWING AS A LEADER

Personal Assessment

To feel that what you have done is worthwhile, you need to see that you have changed or grown as a result of your investment of time and energy. A thoughtful appraisal with or without another person's feedback is the first step in moving forward in growth. You can teach yourself pastoral small group skills. Sharing these insights about yourself with another person is a sure way to grow. Try it out by responding to the following questions:

- ❏ What did I enjoy most about my small group?
- ❏ Where could I have felt more comfortable? Why did I feel uncomfortable?
- ❏ What did I learn about the group that I need to remember?
- ❏ Where did I do well in leading? What did I learn about leading?
- ❏ How well did I apply the **Pocket Principles**?
- ❏ In what way(s) did members relate biblical principles to life? What gave me evidence that they understood and were applying what we were discussing?
- ❏ Did everyone respond at least once to gain investment in the group? Whom will I need to encourage to respond more next time so he or she feels a part of the group?
- ❏ How close did I stick to the allotted time schedule?
- ❏ Who else demonstrated leadership qualities and took responsibility in some way in our first time together?
- ❏ For what am I especially thankful?

TWO

Commitments

Commit—to hold out an expectation; to contract an obligation; to become bound to; to be answerable for; to pledge, take upon oneself, vow.

Commitment requires wanting something badly enough to adopt disciplines in order to achieve it. Olympic athletes' desire to be the best fuels them with the motivation to practice and drill and train for years of their lives. In building a small group, a most important factor is the sharing by participants of their expectations and desires for the group as well as the amount of responsibility each is willing to assume to help the group develop community. These disciplines or agreed-upon investments in the group are called *commitments*.

A commitment to attend on a regular basis is the minimum investment that can be made in keeping a group alive. Investments—such as making a commitment to participate, to help carry responsibility, to share ideas, to care for members, to respond enthusiastically and positively, to support members and to be open to grow—reveal how much an individual wants the small group to be fulfilling and successful. Time and energy invested are major criteria for building community.

At the end of this session, not only will group members be aware of where they need to grow personally, but also of

94

what will be expected of them as a part of this group. Items you may want to come to agreement on during this session include the best time to begin and end, what will be expected regarding attendance and participation, which elements will be included in your time together (e.g., prayer, sharing, study, refreshments) and how responsibilities will be delegated.

As **Group Leader** of this small group experience, *you* have a choice as to which elements will best fit your group, your style of leadership, and your purposes. After you examine the **Session Objectives**, select the activities under each heading with which to begin your community building.

Pocket Principle

1 Discussing expectations and what is needed to meet those expectations provides security, invites responsibility, avoids surprises, and helps each individual feel ownership toward the small group.

Pocket Principle

2 Refreshments can build a group together provided they (1) don't take time from or interrupt the session, (2) don't require the absence of a group member to prepare, and (3) don't become so elaborate that they are unmanageable.

SESSION OBJECTIVES

√ To share expectations and discuss responsibilities to fulfill agreed-upon expectations.

√ To come to an agreement on what commitments each person will make to our group.

√ To help each person target a growth area where he or she wants to change.

√ To declare what kind of group this will be and what disciplines we will adopt to reach that goal.

95

GETTING ACQUAINTED   10–20 minutes

Have a group member read aloud **You Gotta' Wanna'.** Then choose one of the following activities to help create a more comfortable, nonthreatening atmosphere for your small group.

Levels Of Importance

After group members complete the continuums, ask each person to share his or her answers to the following questions:

- ❏ What were you committed to as a child? How did it show?
- ❏ What were you committed to as a youth? What indicated this?
- ❏ What are you committed to as an adult? How do you express your commitment?
- ❏ How have your commitments changed over the years?

Shared Commitment

Ask a group member to read aloud **GroupSpeak.** Point out that sharing expectations of what it means to be a group member and agreeing upon responsibilities that go with membership in the group are foundational for developing a good small group.

Optional—The Cost of Commitment

Explain that there is always a price tag attached to commitment—a price we will pay only if we really want the desired goal. Ask group members to suggest the price attached to the items listed below.

Commitment   **Price Tag**

To lose weight
To become skilled in racquetball
To go to college
To marry
To own a house
To learn a foreign language
To join a small group

Optional — Commitment Is. . . .
Ask group members to complete this sentence: **Commitment is . . .** For example:

❑ Commitment is treating your spouse to dinner (as you promised), even though you're tired and don't feel like going out.
❑ Commitment is putting money toward your kid's braces when you'd rather be saving for a boat.

GAINING INSIGHT   25–30 minutes

Scripture Study
Have group members take turns reading the material in this section. Then discuss these questions:

❑ **What characters in Scripture can you recall who paid a price to please God because of their commitment to Him?** (Moses gave up Egyptian ease. Abraham gave up his country and family. Joseph gave up fleshly pleasures and revenge. Job suffered loss and pain, but remained committed. Hannah gave her son, Samuel, back to God's service. Because of his devotion to God, David denied himself the pleasure of getting even with Saul. Paul experienced loss, beatings, being shipwrecked, poverty, and hunger.)

❑ **What persons in history come to your mind when you think of examples of commitment?** (Abraham Lincoln, Thomas Edison, Patrick Henry, Martin Luther King, Jr., Olympic athletes, musicians and artists who lived in poverty in order to pursue their talents.)

After a group member reads aloud Mark 10:28-30, discuss these questions:

❑ **What do you think "everything" in verse 28 included?** (It probably included their livelihood, their families and the comforts of home, their plans for the future, allegiance to lesser things.)

❑ **What do you think commitment cost those who agreed to a discipling relationship with Jesus?** (Jesus

97

alludes to homes, family relationships, possessions, and jobs. Notice that Jesus doesn't deny or minimize what they have left.)

After group members read John 6:57, 60-62, 66-69, discuss these questions:

❑ **What do these verses suggest about the price tag for commitment?** (It is high, demanding absolutely all. We are to be totally dependent on Him. We live because of Him. He is Lord, and our relationship with Him is what matters.)

❑ **What hard teaching did Jesus give His followers in verse 62?** (He would be removed from them. Being present in the flesh and fulfilling their present fleshly needs was not His goal.)

❑ **Why is it hard even for people today to hear and accept these words?** (We do not like to think of being that dependent on another. We resist making Him Lord and living in that close interaction that requires us to feed [find nourishment in living] on Him. He must be exclusively superior.)

❑ **What do you think made the difference between those who left and those who stayed in verse 66?** (The ones who stayed did not totally understand, but they committed themselves to the Person they knew. Because He was God and because they knew Him, they could trust what He said. Those who did not know Him personally but followed out of ulterior motives could not trust and turned back when His responses did not pass their criteria. They made themselves and what they wanted superior to Him and what He desired.)

❑ **Why do you think having to change affects commitment?** (Notice how the followers' unbelief affected their commitment in verse 66. They didn't want to be committed if they had to change their beliefs.)

❑ **Why do you think Jesus asked the question in verse 67?** (He gave the disciples opportunity to declare affirmatively for Him and thus to take a step in the direction of increasing their faith. Every declared statement of faith leads to more faith.)

Have the group study verses 68-69 and then in their own words, tell the person beside them what Peter is saying.

Reaffirm Your Commitment
Ask several group members to pray, thanking Jesus for His commitment to each group member.

GROWING BY DOING   25–30 minutes

Writing Your Commitment
After everyone has written some things they would be committed to, ask each person to share one thing desired and what it is likely to cost. Items you may want to bring up if not suggested are:

❑ **When can we expect the meeting to start and end?**
❑ **What can we commit to in attendance?**
❑ **What member involvement will we agree to?** (supply refreshments, open home, contact other members, help lead, participate in socials, bring a certain translation of the Bible, participate in answering questions, praying, etc.)
❑ **Will this be an open group where we can bring guests or a closed group for eight weeks where we limit participants to those who are here? What are the advantages and disadvantages of each type of group?**
❑ **How will baby-sitting be arranged?**

Pocket Principle

3 Do not involve group members in baby-sitting where they have to miss out on the group meeting. Scheduling baby-sitting someplace other than the meeting place prevents interruptions and helps group members feel more a part of the group.

❑ **What parts will be included in your group time and how much emphasis on each?** (Sharing, Bible study, experiencing the truth in application, praying for members, eating, recreating.)

❑ **Do we have time and energy to consider a service project which we do together outside the group?**

You may want to decide some of these things ahead of time as leader and share them with the group so all are aware and can decide whether they want to commit to the group. Members in the group may bring up other commitments which are important to them and should be discussed.

Pocket Principle

4 It is important for each person to contribute to the commitment he or she will agree to as a member of this group. If the leader makes all the decisions, it will be the leader's small group and group members will feel less responsible to attend and participate.

Our Small Group Covenant

Summarize your small group's commitments in a short statement. For example, "We commit ourselves to meet together as a group every Tuesday for eight weeks from 7:30 to 9:00 P.M., to share our lives, to talk about what God's Word has to say about the way we live, and to seek to apply that truth to our lives. We agree to care for members by learning each others' names and by seeking to get to know each other individually over the eight weeks we are together. We covenant to be present (except for illness or out of town) and to participate by answering questions and sharing experiences."

It is not necessary to repeat every detail but be sure each person understands what is expected as you covenant to meet together for eight weeks. Encourage each group member to record their covenant in the space provided.

Should a question not discussed here arise later, take time to talk through how the group wants to handle the decision. If group members do not follow through on commitments made here (e.g., they agree to arrive at 7:30 but consistently don't show up until 7:45), bring up the agreement as an objective item and discuss whether the group wants to reaffirm or change their agreement.

Optional—Worship Ideas

Spend some time in worship affirming the small group covenant. Focus on the faithfulness of God in His commitment to us by reading Psalm 89:1-5 and singing "Great Is Thy Faithfulness" or "I Will Sing of the Mercies of the Lord." Recall together or read several of the Lord's promises to us, reminding each other of His faithfulness to carry out what He has promised because He is committed to us. His faithfulness extends to a group of believers who commit themselves to Him, to doing His Word, and to loving each other. Consider promises that will energize and impact the group. For example, "When we gather in His name, He has promised to be there in the midst of us."

Optional—Photo Reminder

Take group photos and provide each person with a copy of the group photo as a reminder to pray for the growth of bonding between group members.

GOING THE SECOND MILE   5 minutes

Group Checkup

Encourage group members to continue affirming the group covenant in a spirit of personal worship and consecration. They can complete the **Going the Second Mile** section on their own.

GROWING AS A LEADER

Personal Assessment

Continue to gain insight into your leadership by examining the following areas with a colleague or in your own personal reflection.

❑ How do I feel about the commitments we've made? Did I share all that I needed to share regarding my expectations?

❑ What is something that being the leader of our group is going to cost me?

101

❏ How can I communicate to the group that I am committed to them? What is a discipline I will need to adopt? How can I let them know of my commitment to them?

❏ How did my leadership in this session reflect my commitment to God's calling me to this position of leadership?

❏ How did my leadership reflect my expectation that everyone be involved in our group?

❏ Where did I see group members taking responsibility for the group's good?

❏ What caused our group to focus on God during this group time? Did we leave with our commitment to Him uppermost?

❏ What did I learn about myself and my leadership style?

❏ What can I plan to do next time to reinforce or change my leadership style?

❏ What did I learn about our group that excites me in terms of its potential?

❏ What leads me to believe that group members feel this is their group, not just mine to lead?

THREE

Relationships

"After being in our group for two years, a man committed suicide. It got the entire group thinking. How could we have helped this gentleman more than we did?"

"Fran and I were the oldest in our group and our family is grown—everybody else had younger children. One of the neat things is that we were able to share some insights and let them know that their families aren't so different."

"The first year a woman in our small group hardly talked at all. She said a couple of things, but she was real guarded and she held herself real tight. In this second year, she has just blossomed. Now she is even involved in getting meals to people and calling people on the phone—a side of her personality we would never have seen without the support she has felt in the small group."

One of the major reasons people join a small group is to get to know others and to feel a sense of belonging. Yet sharing yourself with another can be a scary thing. Small groups are a laboratory for learning how to care and how to share. Most activities in the church do not require us to open ourselves up as real people. It is not usual for us to reveal our needs. It is easier to come across as together and sufficient. Jesus' plan was that His Body be family to one another—that joys and needs be shared—and that we learn to be real with one another. This session places special focus on getting to know one another as special people and learning how to care for each other as members of God's family.

As **Group Leader** of this small group experience, *you* have a choice as to which elements will best fit your group, your style of leadership, and your purposes. After you examine the **Session Objectives,** select the activities under each heading with which to begin your community building. You have many choices.

SESSION OBJECTIVES

√ To know the impact of spending time with others.
√ To realize the importance of sharing yourself and how to do it.
√ To learn from each other.
√ To learn to care for each other and share needs with each other.
√ To bond with others in the group, learning to trust them.

GETTING ACQUAINTED   15–20 minutes

Pocket Principle

1 Sharing the past is the least threatening activity, so begin by asking people to share their histories and move slowly into their present lives.

Have a group member read aloud **To Know Me Is To Love Me.** Then choose one of the following activities to help create a more comfortable, nonthreatening atmosphere for your small group.

Trading Information
Divide into groups of four or six and ask group members to trade information.

Optional—The Real You

Ask group members to think through some things that we could share to let each other know who we are:

☐ A pet peeve or habit
☐ Something you are proud of
☐ A victory you've had
☐ Something you like about yourself
☐ Something you would like to change about yourself
☐ A way that you have seen yourself change
☐ Something you fear

Optional—Getting To Know You

Divide into pairs. Give one partner two minutes to share as many facts as possible about him/herself. Call "time" and ask the other partner to do the same. Then ask the pair to join with another pair. Give this foursome four one minute periods to share with the group as many facts about their partner as they can remember. If you have time, ask each to pick one of the facts and share their feelings about it.

Pocket Principle

2 Feelings indicate who a person is more than facts. Feelings move us deeper and reveal who we really are so whenever possible, ask: How did you feel about that? For example, it is informative to hear, "I was an only child," but more is revealed in responding to, "How did you feel about being an only child?"

Optional—Wanted Posters

Give each person a pencil, a photocopy of the **Wanted Poster** found below, and a straight pin. Have group members fill in the **Poster** and then pin it to their backs. Spend at least 10 minutes milling around the room sharing and reading **Wanted Posters.** If preferred, each may present his or her **Poster** to the whole group so all get to know each other. You may also leave off the name and occupation and seek to guess who created the **Poster** with the remaining information.

WANTED

NAME _____

OCCUPATION _____

FOR

ALWAYS BEING _____

_____

REALLY ENJOYING _____

_____

DESCRIBING HIM/HERSELF AS _____

_____

GREATLY VALUING _____

_____

LIVING BY THE SLOGAN/CONVICTION _____

_____

Pocket Principle

3 Silent members are a threat to the group because people don't know who they are and what they are thinking. Avoid creating silent members by structuring sharing in subgroups of three or four so all can participate.

GAINING INSIGHT   25–30 minutes

Scripture Study

Have group members take turns reading aloud this section as

well as Mark 8:33-37, Luke 9:46-48, John 13:12-14, 14:9-10. Then discuss the following questions.

❏ **What did the Twelve do when they met together?** (It was together they learned who Jesus was. He taught them new lessons and corrected them in front of each other.)

❏ **How did Jesus deal with conflicts in His small group?** (He recognized their interpersonal conflicts and brought them out into the open.)

❏ **What do you see Jesus doing to build trust and concern in the Twelve for each other?** (He caused them to be aware of and to care for one another. It was only natural that after Jesus left, the disciples stood together for what they believed [Acts 2:14].)

Now read Acts 2:42-47 and discuss these questions.

❏ **How does this band of believers reflect togetherness and trust of one another?** (Foundational to giving themselves to one another was their central trust in and focus on God.)

❏ **What is appealing about this group of people?** (Their mutual tie to the same Father knit them together.)

Read what took place in Acts 4:23-35. Then discuss the following questions.

❏ **What qualities were present in this group ministry? What good principles did they exhibit?** (They shared their situation openly, v. 23; believed God and prayed for each other, v. 24; rehearsed God's power, greatness, and control, vv. 24, 27-28; asked for qualities to overcome, v. 29; prayed for evidence of God's power among them, v. 30; all shared in the problem situation as their own, were filled with the Spirit and spoke boldly, v. 31; all shared in material blessings of others, v. 35)

Optional—Questions For Discussion
Ask group members to share their answers to the following questions.

☐ What is attractive to you about this group?

☐ What seems foreign or difficult to you? Why?

☐ Is it easier to share problems, decisions, and dilemmas than to share possessions? Why or why not? Which is easier for you?

☐ What does it mean in verse 32 to be "one in heart and mind"? Does it mean no differences of opinion? Conformity?

☐ Have you ever experienced this oneness among Christians? When?

☐ What helps to develop this kind of trust?

Care Is A Personal Thing

Read and discuss this section carefully. Try to encourage each person to share what "caring" means to him or her. Examine the suggested ways of caring and as a group determine which ones we can agree on for this group.

Pocket Principle

4 Building trust among members takes time. Usually it takes at least three to four sessions for the trust level to develop.

GROWING BY DOING   20–25 minutes

Caring For Us

Divide into twos and threes to talk about specific decisions, dilemmas, or situations that group members have listed. Decide how each needs to be cared for and set up a caring system for the week.

Optional—Project Caring

Talk about ways your group could express care for others in the Body of Christ. For example, the group could exchange childcare, give a half day to repair or clean the home of an elderly person, or serve a month in the church nursery as teams. As individuals, they could set up "getting to know you" dinners, invite other group members to dinner, or offer skills to your group (I offer my skill as an electrician; I'd be glad to make a dessert for someone; I can give two hours of time to share my method of organizing my cabinets). You may want to give each person an offering slip where a member can share his or her name, phone number, and completion of this sentence: **I offer . . .**

Optional—Worship Ideas

Sing some songs about the family of God such as: "We are One in the Bond of Love"; "They Will Know We Are Christians by Our Love"; "This Is My Commandment that You Love One Another." Share some expressions of how God has used the Body of Christ to care for you. Read Acts 4:23-35 again and then pray for specific qualities seen in the passage to be present in the group.

GOING THE SECOND MILE   5 minutes

Group Checkup

Challenge the group to complete the **Going the Second Mile** section on their own. Set up some form of accountability to follow up on caring begun during this group time.

GROWING AS A LEADER

Personal Assessment

Continue to gain insight into your leadership by examining the following areas with a colleague or in your own personal reflection.

Which phrase describes how you feel about the group time?

- ❑ exciting
- ❑ right on target
- ❑ a bit slow
- ❑ informative
- ❑ a learning experience
- ❑ a little uneasy

Think about the members of your group. What do you know about their personalities and needs? Whom do you still need to get to know? How could you plan to do this? Who shows evidence of growth?

What facts did you pick up in this session? What feelings? What changes in lives?

❑ Facts:

❑ Feelings:

❑ Changes:

What's a principle you're learning about leading that you could pass on to new leaders?

I've learned that _____

What did you do in your leading to build a sense of trust in members?

What indicates to you that members feel that this is their group—not your group?

What is one goal you set for yourself as leader to improve the next group time?

Goal: To _____

FOUR

Truth

This is a day of information overload. We are bombarded by truth coming off the press, beamed over the air waves, shared by personal communication, and accompanying of new products. Most of us have more buttons on our VCRs than we know what to do with. We feel guilty when we do not know, but we seem incapable of learning all that is available.

But God has made us hungry to know and understand. His Truth is priority in that knowing and understanding. It is the prerequisite for living the abundant life. Any small group that calls itself Christian must include input from the Lord. The Scriptures are a vital resource, providing guidance, correction, and instruction. But they are not an end in themselves unless we are aiming to produce Pharisees. They are a means to producing disciples who not only know Truth, but practice it. Jesus calls us to, "Go and make disciples . . . teaching them to obey everything I have commanded you" (Matthew 28:19-20).

As **Group Leader** of this small group experience, *you* have a choice as to which elements will best fit your group, your style of leadership, and your purposes. After you examine the **Session Objectives**, select the activities under each heading with which to begin your community building. You have many choices.

SESSION OBJECTIVES

√ To know the importance and necessity of Truth (input from the Lord) in a group session.
√ To be excited about learning biblical Truth.
√ To value the act of learning.
√ To see biblical facts as Truth that should be incarnated in living—not as ends in themselves.
√ To learn something new and choose to practice it in life.

GETTING ACQUAINTED   15–20 minutes

Read aloud **What You Don't Know Can Hurt You.** Then choose one of the following activities to help create a more comfortable, nonthreatening atmosphere for your small group.

Confucious (or Chuck) Says . . .
Have the group complete this exercise and share their response to the question of what they've learned by following the *Confucious* example. For instance, "George says . . . Janet says . . ."

Optional—Questions For Jesus
Explain to the group that at age 12, Jesus dumbfounded the scribes in the Temple with His wisdom and understanding. Persons who heard Jesus asked, "How did this man get such learning?" (John 7:15) Ask: **If you had time with Jesus and could ask Him any content question, what would you like to ask?**

Optional—Facts Learned About Us
Drawing upon sharing that has taken place in your group the previous three sessions, develop a trivia quiz incorporating facts about your group members. For example, Who comes from a family of eleven? Who enjoys skiing and has the scars to prove it? For whom is New York a memorable place and why? Create a handout of this trivia quiz to be answered by teams and then shared, or read the questions directly to the

group and allow them to recall who shared this trivia and its meaning for that person. Mention that one of the benefits of being in a small group is learning new and interesting facts about group members.

GAINING INSIGHT   35–40 minutes
Pocket Principle

1 **If group members are not used to pulling Truth out of Scripture for themselves, you may want to shorten the time and amount of Scripture to be studied.**

Scripture Study
After summarizing this section, divide into subgroups of four and study Matthew 6:19–7:12.

Matthew 6:19-24
Discuss the principles in each of the following contrasts:

❑ **Two Kinds of Treasures** (We need to focus our efforts on what God values and invest in it rather than in the temporary, vulnerable values of now. This value investment will determine what we love and are motivated by.)

❑ **Two Kinds of Eyes** (The condition of the receptor—the eye—affects how much understanding the person has. There are clear receptors and poor receptors which create insight or confusion in the understanding of a person. Openness to truth leads to understanding that pervades all we are and do.)

❑ **Two Kinds of Masters** (Lordship is single-minded. Having two who rule us means we will have to choose allegiance to one or the other because they will work at cross purposes sooner or later. We cannot serve God and anything else.)

Ask group members to share one meaning these principles have for their lives. Then discuss the following questions.

Matthew 6:25-34

❏ **What does Jesus teach about worry?** (We can choose not to worry. If God cares for less valuable parts of His creation, He can be depended upon to care for us. Besides, worry doesn't accomplish anything. People without God worry. If we focus on Him and what He values, we will not waste time stewing over something that might not even happen.)

❏ **What kind of person is Jesus seeking to develop by teaching this?** (A person who trusts the Father, a Parent who not only knows what is needed but is perfectly adequate to supply all that is necessary.)

Have group members share an area in their lives where a promise from this passage could make a difference.

Matthew 7:1-5

❏ **What is Jesus calling us to be in this passage?** (A gracious evaluator and enabler whose attention is focused on correcting the only thing he or she has control over — his or her own conduct and attitudes.)

❏ **Why is this a good rule for healthy living?** (It promotes personal growth and minimizes critical and negative thoughts and statements which frustrate and divide.)

Matthew 7:7-12

❏ **What information do you pick up from this passage?** (God responds to assertiveness and requests. God is not One who withholds good gifts from those who are His. We should treat others the way we would like others to treat us.)

Ask group members to share what teaching in this section encourages them.

Reassemble the group and discuss these bonus questions.

❏ **What did you learn about God in the "worry section"?** (God is aware and responds by providing all we need.)

114

❑ **What did you learn about God in the "judging section"?** (God reciprocates our gracious or severe attitude of evaluation.)

❑ **What did you learn about God in the "asking section"?** (God responds to our pursuit of Him with good gifts.)

Ask a group member to read aloud Matthew 7:24-27. Then ask: **What is the place of Scripture according to these verses?** (Explain that it is to be practiced. The information is to be heard and utilized. The test is not *knowing*, but *knowing and doing*. Those who put into practice the Truth of the Scriptures have stability and strength when stress times come. A Christian small group is vitally interested in what God has to say so it can put what has been learned into practice. God calls foolish the one who hears and does not respond by living according to the Truth.)

Pocket Principle

2 The more you can help persons to be specific in deciding what they will do to practice the Truth, the more likely they are to follow through on their decisions.

GROWING BY DOING   15–20 minutes

Being Wise In Our Individual Lives
Have group members return to subgroups of four and discuss their responses to the Sermon on the Mount. Instruct them to talk through one specific way each person can practice a truth heard in this passage.

Optional—Being Wise In Our Group
Focus on ways your group can become "wise builders." Ask: **What Truth learned from Jesus can we practice together right now? How can we do it?**

Pocket Principle

3 Immediate application of Truth gives stronger motivation for insuring its practice in the lives of group members. Whenever possible, therefore, seek opportunity to put into practice Truth learned.

Optional—Worship Ideas
Sing "Seek Ye First" and read portions of Matthew 5–7, pausing after each excerpt to note what kind of God is revealed by such statements. For example:

❑ 5:16 reveals a God who wants to be glorified.
❑ 5:23-24 reveals a reconciling God who desires harmony.

Spend time praising God for revealing Himself.

GOING THE SECOND MILE   5 minutes

Accountability Check-in
To insure the practice of Truth, set up some type of accountability check-in where group members can:

❑ contact one another between group sessions
❑ trade notecards that declare their intentions
❑ choose another group member to pray for them between group meetings

GROWING AS A LEADER

Personal Assessment
Continue to gain insight into your leadership by examining the following areas with a colleague or in your own personal reflection.

What did I do to help persons put truth into practice? What evidence of this was seen?

How did I help members be specific in their applications?

Which questions asked were particularly helpful?

What are four things our group members learned in this session?

❏ They learned that

❏ They learned to

❏ They learned from

❏ They learned

What did I learn as a leader:

❏ About content?

❏ About process?

❏ About group members?

❏ About my leading?

FIVE

Changes

"Last week's small group time convicted me of a wrongdoing in my life. I had taken a pair of gardening gloves from work and wrapped them up for a Christmas present. I never felt quite right about it and knew I had to do something to correct my mistake. The next day I bought two pair of gloves, one to replace the pair I had taken and one to replace a pair I received last year from another employee. Because of the small group study I realized that my faith must affect my lifestyle."

The word *change* holds both a sense of promise as well as a sense of threat. It happens slowly, but constantly. Sometimes it takes place unconsciously and, at other times, it is deliberately planned. The presence of growth indicates life while its absence indicates death. Change in the direction of likeness to Christ is the goal of our maturing. Awareness of growth and change is encouraging. For the child who sees the measurements on the wall chart change or the adult who succeeds in mastering a new job skill, growth is energizing.

Small groups provide excellent climates for personal growth. As we continue in this study, we need to take time to focus on our growth—to affirm and reassess for the final three weeks of this commitment as well as celebrate that growth. As **Group Leader** of this small group experience, *you* have a

118

choice as to which elements will best fit your group, your style of leadership, and your purposes. After you examine the **Session Objectives,** select the activities under each heading with which to begin your community building.

SESSION OBJECTIVES

√ To recognize growth and change in our lives.
√ To desire further transformation in Christlikeness.
√ To encourage others in their growth as witnessed in the group.
√ To identify and share with the group where further desired changes are to be made.

GETTING ACQUAINTED   15–20 minutes

Have a group member read aloud **I'm Growing.** Then choose one of the following activities to help create a more comfortable, nonthreatening atmosphere for the first meeting of your small group.

I Usta Think
After discussing the questions, ask group members to share the growth that has taken place in their thinking by using the following phrase: **I usta think . . . but now I know . . .**

Optional—Magic Wand
Explain that many people today dream of winning the lottery and think of all the changes that winning would produce in their lives. Cinderella had a fairy godmother who granted her special gifts. Aladdin's lamp supposedly contained a genie who would grant wishes. Ask: **Imagine you have been given the capacity to change. What is one thing you would change about (1) your work, (2) people around you, (3) yourself.**

Pocket Principle

1 Change most often takes place in a small group setting where there is security, love, and trust built among members

119

who are willing to challenge as well as encourage one another.

GAINING INSIGHT   20–25 minutes

Scripture Study

After reading this first section and working through the questions, ask each group member to share what he or she remembers with the person beside him or her for the next 5–7 minutes.

Read aloud the Scriptures and discuss what was expected to prompt growth in each of these instances.

John 14:8-9

❏ **What prompted growth in this situation?** (Jesus' answer betrays His surprise, as though Philip should have already learned this basic Truth. All Jesus said and did was to show His followers who He was and to generate a change in their attitudes and actions because they had learned He was God.)

John 10:36-38

❏ **What prompted growth in this situation?** ("Believing the miracles" provided an openness that would lead to understanding and receiving who Jesus was—One with God. What happens to us—the circumstances and God's intervention in our lives—is often a growth opportunity to discover the deeper truths of who He is. God expects we will grow from going through these experiences.)

Mark 6:30-44

❏ **What prompted growth in this situation?** (The 5,000 hungry listeners gave Jesus an opportunity to present to the disciples the truth about who He was.)

Pocket Principle

2 Asking another group member to read is a good way to involve silent members, but make certain the person feels comfortable reading aloud and can do it accurately and with meaning.

Mark 6:45-52

❏ **What prompted growth in this situation?** (A crisis situation filled with terror was resolved by recognizing His presence with them. His presence is adequate to give courage. Mark added a reason as to why the disciples hadn't grown when they experienced this situation in verse 52.)

❏ **This event was a test of what Jesus had sought to teach the disciples when He fed the 5,000. What did He want them to recognize about Himself?** (He is God and thus sufficient for any situation—feeding thousands of hungry people or calming high winds. His presence brings hope to any situation.)

Mark 8:1-10

❏ **What prompted growth in this situation?** (Again, Jesus showed Himself more than adequate to provide satisfaction for the needs of people. He was Master of the situation—divine Son of God. Twice He showed Himself Provider in this arena.)

Mark 8:14-21

❏ **What was the disciples' concern?** (v. 16) (The lack of food for their need.)

❏ **Why was it unbelievable to Jesus that they would struggle with this issue?** (vv. 18-20) (They wouldn't go hungry. He had supplied more bread than they needed twice.)

❏ **Of what does Jesus accuse the disciples that prevents their growth in understanding?** (vv. 17-18) (hardened, unbelieving hearts; having eyes and ears but not allowing them to do what they are designed to do.)

Often a circumstance becomes an opportunity to grow when we approach it with *What is God teaching me about Himself in this situation?* or *How does remembering God's help in the past enable me to believe Him for this present situation?* Use these questions to help group members determine what specific areas of their lives need growth and change.

GROWING BY DOING   15–20 minutes

Present Learning Opportunity

In pairs, talk about present situations in which God is teaching you about Himself, resulting in growth. Close by praying for areas where each person has expressed a need to grow.

Optional—Sharing "Bread" Stories

Share with the whole group a time when God supplied something you needed and proved Himself to be God in your life. How did this "miracle" lead you to understand and know Him better?

Optional—Worship Ideas

Make your worship time an exciting time of giving praise for changes in persons, situations, perspectives, and/or abilities. Give each person an outline of a plant. As each member shares ways he or she personally has grown, or how the group has grown, draw a leaf on the plant, recording the person's name and the area of growth identified. This leafy plant becomes the pictorial expression of the fruit produced by God in persons in the group. Send it home with group members to remind them to give thanks for evidences of change and progress.

GOING THE SECOND MILE   5 minutes

Take Time To Give Thanks

Remind group members of the areas where they have experienced growth. Encourage each person to take time at each meal to thank God for one of the specific growth evidences mentioned by a group member.

GROWING AS A LEADER

Prayer Cards

A good leader is constantly monitoring where persons in the group are—spiritually, socially, personally, emotionally. Set up your own list of members and think through where you have seen each person grow. Use this list as a prayer card to pray for specific growth in the lives of individual members.

122

SIX

Caring

Hallmark prides itself on being the choice of those who "care enough to send the very best." Although the sale of cards is up, many observers of society are concerned that we have become a nation of non-carers. Psychologists have cited the senseless killing of Kitty Genovese, who was repeatedly stabbed while onlookers heard her screams and did nothing. The muggings, the plight of the homeless, and the poverty of the single parent are appalling in the wealthiest nation on earth. The nightly recital of daily catastrophes in the news has lowered our care decibel. We are confronted with more relationships in a two week period than our grandparents were in a lifetime. All these factors and more make for an impersonal world. At the same time, we are longing for care. The singles' bars, the hunger for relationships, the weekly visits to the counselor, the personal ads, and more trumpet our need for knowing someone cares.

Small groups can become those communities of care that provide strength and give believers the acceptance they do not find elsewhere. As **Group Leader** of this small group experience, *you* have a choice as to which elements will best fit your group, your style of leadership, and your purposes. After you examine the **Session Objectives**, select the activities under each heading with which to begin your community building.

SESSION OBJECTIVES

√ To know what a "caring group" involves.
√ To be motivated to express care.
√ To discover new dimensions of caring in Scripture.
√ To commit ourselves to caring in specific ways.

GETTING ACQUAINTED   20–30 minutes

Have a group member read aloud **Try It, You'll Like It.** Then choose one of the following activities to help create a more comfortable, nonthreatening atmosphere for your small group.

Care Packages
After discussing the questions in this section, ask your group to share how they would complete the following sentence: **A time when I really experienced feeling cared for in this group was when . . .**

Optional — Care Agenda
Explain that because people experience care in many different ways, we need to know what each group member prefers when it comes to expressing care. Ask each person to list three or four things that say "care" to him or her and then share the list with another group member. Prime the pump by mentioning the following items:

❏ Receiving a note of appreciation
❏ Experiencing someone offering to pray for me
❏ Getting a phone call from a group member
❏ Spending time with another group member
❏ Someone listening to me
❏ Evidence that a person knows what I like and has taken the time and effort to do that
❏ A hug or a squeeze that reassures me that I am loved
❏ An unexpected gift

Optional — A Caring Group
Discuss what a caring group would look like. Ask: **What would you expect from such a group? Which of these**

expectations do you think is realistic for our current group? In what specific ways have you seen care exercised in our group thus far?

If your group is open to different methods, give each twosome a sheet of newsprint and ask each person to draw stick figures depicting several ways of caring that are possible for the group. Share these sheets with the whole group and decide which "caring portraits" you want to adopt as a group.

Pocket Principle

1 Most adults are used to verbal forms of expressing ideas and feelings. However, fresh insights and meaningful sharing can be gained by introducing out of the ordinary techniques. When utilizing drawings, assure participants that your goal is not artistic excellence, but rather fresh expressions of ideas. Sharing a sample stick figure drawing of your own helps free up adults to use a different medium of expression.

Who Cares!
Work through this section together, discussing the following questions.

❑ **What evidences of lack of caring have come to your awareness? How have we become an impersonal society?** (Group members may suggest such items as environmental issues where we shirk responsibility for caring for the next generation and its need of resources or the plight of the homeless, the poverty dwellers, the single parent, the unjustly treated where human beings are doomed to live their whole lives as second class citizens. Or the group may come up with evidences of impersonalness such as the disposable person who is discarded from a job or a relationship because he or she is seen as too old, too ineffective, too predictable, too costly to maintain.)

Lead your group in uncovering some of these accepted phenomena that betray our deterioration of caring and the distancing of persons from feelings of care. To stimulate their thinking you may wish to bring in newspapers and current events magazines which reveal today's censored feeling of care for persons.

❑ **What are some understandable reasons for our not finding it necessary to feel with and for others if we want to survive in our present world?** (The group may suggest such reasons as the sheer number of caring situations they are exposed to; the nightly bombardment of need as reflected in the news stories from around the globe; the isolation from personal contact with specific persons in need—their stories become only informational statistics, not causes for personal concern. Other aspects are the current emphasis on self-advancement and preservation at the expense of feeling concern for another; the goal of self-fulfillment and taking care of yourself as emphasized by modern psychology; the American ideal of individualism—standing on your own two feet needing nobody; the fear of vulnerability and how it can be used against you.)

 ## GAINING INSIGHT   30 minutes

Scripture Study
Encourage the group to put together what they know about the disciples and what it must have been like to be in a group discipled by Jesus as people who needed caring for surrounded Him. Ask: **What factors would have made it difficult for the disciples to become a group that cared for each other?**

Share that it might have been easier for James and John to care for Peter and Andrew because they were old fishing buddies from Capernaum. It might have been hard to understand and care for those who were different in temperament and background. Thomas' exactness could have been frustrating while Peter's boldness could have been obnoxious. Matthew's perspectives as a tax collector for Rome would have been opposite opinions of Simon the Zealot who was hoping for the overthrow of Rome and Jewish reinstatement of power.

126

Ask various group members to assume the roles of James, John, Jesus, and the other disciples as they read aloud the parts of the characters and the narrator in Mark 10:35-45. After role players have described what emotions they felt as they read their parts, discuss the following questions.

❑ **How do you see Jesus showing care for James and John? How does He care for the other disciples?** (He gives opportunity for them to realize and admit their own inadequacy by asking the question, "Can you drink the cup I drink?" When they persist in their request, He does not shame nor scoff at them but gives further insight regarding the giving of places in the new kingdom. Jesus cared for the "left-out ones" by helping them learn from their anger and jealousy.)

❑ **What do you think the phrase "they became indignant with James and John" means?** (They became incensed at their exclusiveness and boldness that seemed selfish in it's focus.)

❑ **How did Jesus indicate that this was a caring issue for the whole group? Why is it caring to face group issues head on?** (He called them together to deal upfront with their feelings. Facing an issue means working it through so it doesn't simmer and create division. Confronting is really "care-fronting" because it says our feelings are important. Let's understand each other.)

❑ **How is a desire for greatness among others an uncaring attitude?** (This attitude focuses on self and self's promotion, not on caring for others' needs. The result of caring for the good of others is greatness.)

❑ **How did Jesus describe the way Gentiles built relationships? How are Jesus followers to be different?** (Culture said, "Lord it over, show authority." Jesus' followers are to lift up others and see that they are fulfilled. There is a voluntary "coming under" to exalt another's needs.)

Summarize this section by asking the group what principles for nurturing care among believers they would list from this incident in Mark 10. Some principles might include:

❑ Face attitudes that could divide the group.
❑ Be gracious in giving insight to another person.
❑ Ask questions wherever possible.
❑ See how Jesus modeled truth in a similar situation.
❑ Help another to find fulfillment by voluntarily placing yourself at his or her service.
❑ Make group conflict a learning situation for the group.
❑ Call the group to focus on shared loyalties to Jesus rather than on individual rightness or wrongness.

Ask a member to read aloud John 13:2-17 where a model of caring is given in verses 2-11. Then discuss the following questions.

❑ **In what ways do you see Jesus demonstrating care here?** (Jesus focused on their needs instead of His position and impending needs. He gently worked through resistance with Peter. He gave care to Judas, knowing it would not be reciprocated.)

❑ **How does Jesus call the disciples to henceforth care for one another in John 13?** (He calls them to voluntarily give up the rights that go with position and serve one another by observing and then ministering to one another. This could be in the area of physical supply, encouraging spirits, giving insight, supporting another's ministry with presence and abilities. The disciples in Acts 2 stood up with Peter when he spoke to the large crowd at Pentecost. Mention that we do not read of the disciples literally washing each other's feet hereafter, although that is not outside the realm of possibility.)

Ask group members to discuss what opportunities we have to care for each other. Summarize by asking the group what principles for caregiving are found in John 13. Some principles might include:

❑ Cultivate awareness of what others need.
❑ Initiate care whether others respond or not.
❑ Don't force your "care" on another.

❏ Be a teaching model of ways to care.

Ask the group to look back over the principles they have gleaned from seeing Jesus cultivate care among His disciples and restate those principles as guidelines for their own lives.

Optional—Additional Examples of Caring

If you have time, you may want to look briefly at two more passages. The first is Luke 24:13-35. After reading these verses, ask: **How did the Emmaus disciples care for the 11 disciples who remained locked in a room in fear in Jerusalem? (vv. 33-35)**

Another situation is found in Luke 22:31-32 at the prediction of Peter's denial. Ask a group member to read these verses. Then ask: **What principle of caring do you find here on the part of Jesus in regard to Peter? How can our failures become a source of care for others?**

GROWING BY DOING   25–30 minutes

Caring Among Us

Share your responses to the questions. To make your caring practical, ask each person to write down an area in which he or she needs care and ways that care could be expressed. After dividing into twos, ask partners to exchange responses and become "care buddies" to follow up on caring for each other.

Pocket Principle

2 Following through on caring is essential to growth. Talking about caring is cheap. Be sure to present several levels of how care can be expressed, so no one feels pushed into doing something for which he or she is not ready. If participants suggest the ways they are ready to care, they are more likely to follow through.

Optional—Worship Ideas

Celebrate the care God gives to His own. Read an excerpt from Margery Williams' children's classic, *The Velveteen Rab-*

bit (Doubleday and Company, 1975) which depicts unconditional acceptance in caring (Chapter 1, beginning with "The Skin Horse had lived longer. . . ." and ending with "once you are Real you can't be ugly, except to people who don't understand.") Discuss how the story reflects the kind of love God has for us. Ask: **In what ways does this become a word picture that reflects how God's loving care is given to us?**

Read aloud Psalm 25, an expression of how the psalmist felt God's care in his life. Suggest that group members let God's caring ways refresh them as they listen to you read. Then sing one or more of the following songs that express our care for one another: "God Will Take Care of You," "In His Time," "Blest Be The Tie That Binds," and "We Are One in the Bond of Love."

Close by celebrating God's care in specific ways using this phrase in praise and prayer: **"Lord, You cared and You..."**

GOING THE SECOND MILE   5 minutes

Care Card
Give each person a Care Card reminder—a label or sticker with the words "I Care!" on it. Encourage group members to follow up on caring for their care buddies chosen earlier. Urge each person to make contact before the group meets again. Ask everyone to be prepared to talk about his or her caring experience at the beginning of next meeting.

GROWING AS A LEADER

Personal Assessment
Continue to gain insight into your leadership by examining the following areas with a colleague or in your own personal reflection.

How do you assess the caring that goes on in our group?

What have you deliberately tried to model for them to imitate?

Who is someone you would guess feels left out or uncared for in our group?

How could you generate care for this person? Through another member? On your own?

How does the preparation and careful handling of your leadership position exhibit care of the persons in your group?

How do you think each would describe being cared for by you or by another in the group?

What's one caring aspect that you plan to build into the group in the remaining times you are together? How do you plan to do that?

SEVEN

Service

Upon purchasing a new appliance or piece of equipment we expect all the parts to be included and in good working order. This is vital to the effective functioning of the purchased item.

God gives us His formula for the body of Christ that He has created. Small groups are one of the best situations for discovering the working order of the body. God has given each one of us gifts that are useful for the whole group.

What we have been given cannot be spent on ourselves, but is revealed in the process of interacting in the Body of Christ. Small groups become laboratories for exciting discoveries and occasions of affirmation and confirmation. We become ministers to one another, equipping each other as God gives us insight and abilities. The variety of gifts is characteristic of His Spirit among us. We grow as each member fulfills an assigned function from God. We are a team, playing different positions, but bent on the same outcome.

As **Group Leader** of this small group experience, *you* have a choice as to which elements will best fit your group, your style of leadership, and your purposes. After you examine the **Session Objectives**, select the activities under each heading with which to begin your community building.

SESSION OBJECTIVES

√ To become aware of each person's special contribution to the body of Christ.

√ To affirm the uniqueness of one another and each person's special ability.

√ To want to contribute giftedness that God has entrusted to individuals for the good of all.

√ To plan ways to serve that utilize the abilities of all.

GETTING ACQUAINTED   20–30 minutes

Have a group member read aloud **Made For The Body.** Then choose one of the following activities to help create a more comfortable, nonthreatening atmosphere for the first meeting of your small group.

What Is Your Opinion?

After discussing the first two questions, ask group members to mark and discuss their opinions about spiritual gifts.

Optional — The Medium Is The Message

Enlarge (if possible) and Xerox Romans 12:3-8, 1 Corinthians 12:4-30, and Ephesians 4:4-16. Paste these passages on cardboard and cut into enough jig-saw puzzle pieces for everyone in your group to have one. Distribute these pieces to group members and ask them to piece together their puzzles. Each puzzle group should then discuss this clue: **The medium is the message.**

Ask group members to come back from each of the three groups with a principle they think is the message of their particular Scripture. Their responses may include such principles as: "Everyone is needed to complete the whole;" "All must contribute for the project to be complete;" "We function best when we function together;" "Each is different but the same."

Pocket Principle

1 The purpose here is not to argue over issues nor to display superior insight. It is important that each person's opinion be valued and that each person feel free to give an opinion. Sometimes dividing the group into smaller units frees persons to share what they think.

Optional—Spiritual Gift Inventory

You may wish to order a spiritual gifts inventory or assessment to administer in your group. One of the better ones is Bruce L. Bugbee's *Networking* (Charles E. Fuller Institute).

GAINING INSIGHT   30 minutes

Let's Build Something

For this activity, choose a project (cabin, nursery, church, garage, etc.) that will be relevant to your group. Discuss what kinds of assumptions and/or thoughts could sidetrack the project.

Scripture Study

Have the group read Acts 6. Discuss the following questions.

❑ **In this situation what need arose in the disciples' group that forced them to call on others for help?** (Help was needed by widows who had no one to care for them.)

❑ **How would you describe the group function that took place in this passage?** (The group was given responsibility for the problem.)

❑ **What do the when, the who, and the what in Acts 6:1 add to this situation?** (The church was continuing to grow, but this gave rise to inevitable problems. The two groups of Jews brought different cultures, languages, views on Jewish customs, etc. to the fellowship. Because the widows had no one to care for them, they became the church's responsibility.)

❑ **In the face of these complaints, what assessment did the disciples make?** (They had a ministry to which God had called them, and they did not want to hinder it by getting involved in additional responsibilities.)

❑ **What solution did they come up with?** (With their supervisory skills they organized a plan to give the people a say in solving their own problem.)

❑ **What were the qualities needed by a potential candidate to be chosen for service by the disciples?** (The candidates were to be full of the Spirit and wisdom.)

❑ **What gift of service did the Twelve offer to the group?** (They said they would be responsible for prayer and the ministry of the Word.)

❑ **What did the disciples observe in Stephen that caused them to choose him?** (Stephen must have been full of the Spirit and wisdom, as mentioned in verse 3. However, he is also described as a man full of faith and of the Holy Spirit in verse 5.)

❑ **What further role did the Twelve have in regard to these chosen men?** (The disciples were responsible for praying for and laying on of hands.)

❑ **Why would they pray for and lay hands on those who would distribute food to hungry widows?** (The disciples blessed and commissioned the men who had exhibited the ability to fulfill those responsibilities.)

❑ **What does this tell you about the role these folks had as they contributed their abilities to the group?** (The disciples' act of prayer and laying on of hands indicates the importance they felt about this branch of their ministry.)

❑ **What was the result of everyone contributing what was given to him or her for the good of all?** (The church continued to grow rapidly as the Word of God spread, and the priests in church leadership became more obedient.)

135

❑ **How does the response in Acts 6 illustrate the body concept found in 1 Corinthians 12:7 and Ephesians 4:16?** (Everyone contributed what God had given so that the whole church benefited.)

Read 1 Corinthians 12:12-21, 24b-27 and discuss the following two questions.

❑ **What are two main principles you find in the passage?** (God is responsible for giving abilities and placing persons with different responsibilities in the same groups. He caused us to need each other so we wouldn't be divided in competition or in looking down on another. One's pain is the pain of all.)

Discuss what principles in this passage are also illustrated in Acts 6. Be sure to note that both the Greeks and the Aramaic-speaking Jews were part of Christ's body. They impacted and were responsible for each other. In the same way, the Twelve, the other disciples, the widows, and the complainers were all part of Christ's body. One person's role was not more important or less significant than another person's role.

Ask group members how they see these principles operating in our small group.

Pocket Principle

2 If your group is not experienced or comfortable with pulling principles from Scripture, make it easier by listing the above principles and others and asking them to find their source in the cited passage. Or lead your group with such questions as, "What is said about division being eliminated?" and "Who is responsible for giving abilities?"

 GROWING BY DOING   15–20 minutes

Who's Who

It is important that each person see his or her contribution to the body of Christ (your small group). Structure this activity so that everyone is included or mentioned. Explain that in some instances, we may have several names that fit well under the described ability. Encourage the group to add their own descriptions.

Pocket Principle

3 Because some people are not that familiar with the essence of biblical gifts, you may want to stick with ordinary terms, recognizing skills and natural inclinations. That way, everyone feels free to participate even if they don't know the categories of gifts. For example, you could say, "This person seems really at home doing . . ."

Optional—Gift Users
Discuss the following questions.

❑ How do you see different peoples' abilities being used here in this group?

❑ What abilities have you seen grow or be discovered in your group?

❑ How do you see these abilities being used effectively in the weekday job to which persons have been called?

❑ How does the effective use of this ability serve as a way to call others to Christ?

Optional—Worship Ideas
After talking about various identified strengths in group members, respond as the Twelve did in Acts 6 by praying and laying hands on persons to be used of God to equip and nurture the growth of the Body of Christ.

Songs of worship could focus on our relatedness in Christ, such as "We Are One In The Bond of Love," "We Are One In The Spirit," "Blessed Be The Tie That Binds" or on the Giver of good gifts such as "Father, We Adore You." Close with each person sharing with another, "You are God's gift to the Body" in the same way as "passing the peace" to another.

137

GOING THE SECOND MILE 5 minutes

Personal Checkup

Challenge the group to complete the **Going the Second Mile** section on their own. Encourage group members to put their giftedness into action during the coming week.

GROWING AS A LEADER

Personal Assessment

Continue to gain insight into your leadership by examining the following areas with a colleague or in your own personal reflection.

What would you list as your own gifts and abilities?

How can your leadership incorporate the special abilities given to others in your group?

What could they do that you are currently doing?

EIGHT

Celebration

Christian small groups have Christ at their center. Therefore even though we may move on to new relationships in other small groups, we still have a bonding with persons in this group. We are related to the same Christ and, therefore, related to each other as forever family.

Group times with believers here are temporary and but a taste of what is to come when we sit down with the Lamb at the center of our celebration. But they do give us a glimpse of community which we will one day share in eternity. The final session in a series is an occasion to celebrate and to move on.

We celebrate what God has done in our midst. We celebrate what we have discovered of Him. We celebrate who we have become. We celebrate the glimpses of God-designed community. We celebrate how we have grown so that we are now able and ready to move on to new issues and growth areas. This is an occasion to look back and remember and to look forward and rejoice. The culmination of the ages will be a grand celebration where we reflect on what God has done and anticipate kingdom living ahead. So, practice for the grand finale. Every ending is opportunity for praise of God and for a new beginning of moving on with God. Celebrate the God of your group. Celebrate His being among you!

As **Group Leader** of this small group experience, *you* have a choice as to which elements will best fit your group, your style of leadership, and your purposes. After you examine the **Session Objectives,** select the activities under each heading with which to begin your community building.

You may wish to incorporate some special time of eating together as part of your celebration—a potluck or make-your-own sundae feast. Adjust your schedule accordingly so that persons have time to share as well as eat.

SESSION OBJECTIVES

√ To recognize ways that Jesus has worked within our group.

√ To realize the uniqueness of this group because Jesus was present.

√ To verbalize joys and gains in having been together.

√ To identify what has been important in this group experience.

√ To take steps to increase the satisfaction and effectiveness of our next group study.

GETTING ACQUAINTED   20–30 minutes

Pocket Principle

1 Make this a festive occasion. You have reached a milestone in completing this study. It is important that people look back and rejoice over specific gains and plan ahead incorporating what has become valuable to them.

Have a group member read aloud **God With Us.** Then choose one of the following activities to help create a more comfortable, nonthreatening atmosphere for your small group.

140

It Pays To Advertise

By twos and threes ask members to write an ad for the group. Allow a few minutes to create the ad and then ask each twosome to read what they've written. Look for any patterns or often repeated elements which seem to characterize your group and comment on these. If some prefer to be artistic, provide newsprint, marking pens, and scissors for them to create a poster depicting the character of your group.

Memorable Moments

After allowing a few moments for group members to think, interview each person about some memorable moments in your group's history. If your group has a flair for drama, they may choose to do a mime or to act out several scenes that capsulize the significant events in your time together. You may want to list these moments ahead of time and then assign several scenes to different group members to act out in charade fashion while the others attempt to identify the scene.

Optional—How'd We Do?

Ask group members to evaluate the group time by completing the following sentences.

❏ **A word that describes this group for me is . . .**

❏ **Something I've experienced here is . . .**

❏ **What I have enjoyed about being in this group is . . .**

❏ **Something that surprised me about this group was . . .**

❏ **One benefit I've gained from this group is . . .**

Ask members to share with the whole group one or two of the above items. You may want to incorporate this activity with your praise and worship time at the end of the session.

GAINING INSIGHT   25–30 minutes

Scripture Study

Divide the group into two teams, giving each a passage to study. Instruct the teams to discover what impact Jesus' presence had on the small group in each section of Scripture. Point out that the Scripture has been divided into roles since there is so much dialogue. Assign roles to group members to make the reading more interesting. When the two teams have finished sharing, reassemble the group and ask each team to share their insights. Summarize by asking: **What impresses you about Jesus as a "group member" in each of these situations?**

Pocket Principle

2 To ensure maximum benefit from this Scripture study, prepare another person or two ahead of time to lead questions in a subgroup and to help other group members realize the application of the truths in Scripture.

 GROWING BY DOING   15–20 minutes

My Testimony

Because Jesus has been present in your group, ask group members to share who Jesus is and what He has done in and through the group. Begin this time by sharing your own thoughts.

Optional—He Is Here

Have group members use the following phrase to share what impact Jesus has had on their lives through this group: **Because He was in our midst I . . .**

Thank-You God

Ask group members to spend a few minutes writing a thank-You note to God.

Pocket Principle

3 As Group Leader, be on the lookout for potential "willing to care for others" kind of people whom you can begin to equip for leadership. If you have already approached someone to begin to work with you, this last session is a good time to

make group members aware of his or her role in the group.

Optional—Worship Ideas

Use comments and reflection times from earlier in the session to now become praise and offerings of thanksgiving to God. Remember and then give thanks. Make your worship God-centered, rather than focusing on praising group members. Sing your favorite praise songs. A good theme song about the presence of Jesus is "He is here, He is here, He is moving among us." You may want to set a chair in your group to remind you of the unseen but felt presence of Jesus. Celebrate His being there.

GOING THE SECOND MILE   5 minutes

Share Some Pleasant Words

Challenge the group to complete the **Going the Second Mile** section on their own. Encourage group members to follow through on encouraging each other.

Optional—Moving On

Where do we go from here? The end of this session is a good time for each person to talk about what has become very important to him or her in our group process. Ask: **What is it that we have learned and want to be sure to keep as a part of our group time together? What do we want to change for the next study because of what we've learned?**

GROWING AS A LEADER

Personal Assessment

Reflecting back over the eight sessions, what have been some of your greatest satisfactions?

What has been an encouragement to you in your own leadership development?

143

In what ways has the group measured up to your own expectations?

In what ways have you sought to grow leaders within this group?

What will be a new step you want to take in learning leadership within a small group?

What's one thing you will do differently next time around?